Book cover design by Temi Coker.

ISBN (paperback): 9781687538703

www.amandaapittman.com
www.confidentwomanco.com

CHANGE.

Shed What Was Never You to Reveal Who You've Always Been

AMANDA PITTMAN

DEDICATION

To my beautiful baby girl, Lily Blair.

If I could impact every woman in the world yet I have neglected to impact you, then I have failed. While I don't have the capacity to be the perfect mother, I will try my hardest to set before you the best example of a confident woman that I possibly can.

You are my World-Changer. I pray that you step into your authority as a bold woman of God. May you know your inherent, unchanging value. May you unapologetically use your voice and commission others to do the same. I give you permission to stand on my shoulders and do even more than I ever do. Never shrink. Never question. Never doubt. Just do what you were created to do— change the world.

The Life Cycle of CHANGE

Preface

Here's to the woman who feels trapped. You're the visionary, the leader, the trendsetter, and the pioneer. You're strong, courageous, brave, and bold. You have big dreams, big plans, and big goals. But you're hindered by faulty mindsets and beliefs, triggering pains and regrets, old wounds and scars, useless habits and rituals, and debilitating fear. You place a sacrifice on the altar of change, only to take it back when things get uncomfortable. You step out in faith in the name of change, only to shrink when people start talking about you. You decide to use your voice for good, but then you silence yourself in the face of pressure. Who you are on the outside is trapping who you are on the inside. You're ready to shed away the garment of shame and insecurity that you've worn. You're ready to reveal the confident woman you have always been. You're ready to impact the world through the power of Jesus Christ. You're ready to *change*.

 I've been there: bound to my bruises; married to my mentalities; enslaved to my sin. I've questioned my purpose and calling, wondering why I was even put here on this earth; wondering if I would reach my potential. I've felt like a stranger in my own body—attuned to the radiant, glimmering *inner me* while held hostage by the stagnant, stubborn *outer me*. God has walked me through a miraculous journey of spiritual, mental, emotional, and physical healing. I've discovered the power of my own gifts, talents, abilities, peronality and experiences. I've been empowered by the Holy Spirit to commission others. I've shed off what once held me back and stepped into the woman I was born again to be. I am going to teach you the process to do the same. This is called *The Life Cycle of Change*.

The Life Cycle of Change is comprised of four stages:

Stage One: *Belong*
Stage Two: *Shed*
Stage Three: *Develop*
Stage Four: *Change*

These four stages coincide with the life cycle of a butterfly. A butterfly does not grow from a smaller, child butterfly to a larger, adult butterfly. The insect actually hatches from its egg as a caterpillar. That caterpillar spends its time eating, growing and shedding its skin. When it reaches maturation, that caterpillar enters the pupa stage, where it encases itself in its own protective shell as it develops and transforms, seemingly into a new creature. When it emerges from the chrysalis, the creature is no longer a caterpillar, but is now a dazzling, beaming butterfly. That butterfly is purposed to fly, pollinate flowers, and produce more butterflies. While a butterfly goes through metamorphosis and seemingly becomes a "new creature," let it be known that even while the caterpillar was in egg form, it was always destined to be a butterfly.

In the same way, when we're born again as children of God, it may take us time to change. It takes us time to come out of our shell and embrace a new way of life. We may see other believers flying, wondering why we're still eating, crawling and shedding. We undergo a time of being covered and hidden as we discover our gifts, develop our gifts, and transform. Finally, we emerge from that secret place and spread our beautiful wings for all the world to see. We begin operating in leadership, we develop others, walk in our calling, speak with authority, and navigate our lives with confidence. We exude love, joy, peace, patience, kindness, goodness, faithfulness, gentleness and self-control. We unapologetically impact our spheres and create change in others. The transformation is so striking that everyone sees it. It appears as if we have changed. It may look as if we've arrived. What has actually taken place is that we simply mature into the fullness of what we were born to be.

As you read this book, understand that every stage applies to you. While we all undergo every stage of The Life Cycle of Change at the same time, there is almost always one stage in which our efforts are focused on during a specific time in our lives. You're not meant to remain a caterpillar forever; this system equips you to mature into the next level in your walk with Christ. Apply the tools and truths provided to you in every stage that you find yourself in. The Life Cycle of Change is a framework for the Christian walk that, if implemented across the globe, will bring heaven to earth. If you implement the biblical strategies of growth during each stage of your life, you will see change. You'll emerge into a woman who has the confidence and the character to sustain her calling. The Life Cycle of Change is a duplicatable system that can not only be applied to your life, but also be applied to lives of those you disciple, to the women in your small group, to the children in your home, and so much more. It may take time to do, but it is doable. It requires change, but the change is worth it.

The Life Cycle of CHANGE
Table of Contents

STAGE ONE

BELONG

CHOSEN AT CHURCH CAMP

As I looked around, it was hard to believe where I was. I was the only brown girl surrounded by popular, white, rich girls who packed twice as much luggage as I had. When I arrived, me and all the other 12-year-olds girls were told to pick our beds in a massive air-conditioned room filled with over 20 bunk beds. We shared one huge bathroom. *Will I have to shower around these girls?* I thought to myself, cringing on the inside. The cool girls all rolled up their sleeves and the bottoms of their t-shirts, cinching it to their petite frame. They would freely dress and undress, unashamed by their slim, perfect bodies.

As they talked about boys, they did their skincare routine in the mirror with several name-brand products. I didn't have any skincare products, let alone a skincare routine. I watched them brush their teeth with electric toothbrushes, embarrassed of my cheap manual toothbrush. I watched as they flipped their sleek, straight hair into ponytails, pigtails, and french braids. I just tried to pull my hair into a puffy ponytail, slicking it down with water in attempts to keep the

3

emerging frizzies from making me any more unsightly. I couldn't look or feel any more different.

I felt ashamed to have a small bag packed with granny panties, out-of-style and ill-fitting hand-me-down clothes, an ugly one-piece bathing suit, and a pair of white, oversized pajama pants. When the other girls got ready in the mirror, I saw flat stomachs, long legs dressed in cut-off short shorts, brand new sneakers, and fashion flip flops. I was a short, stumpy brown girl with ill-fitting pants, old shoes, fuzzy-frizzy hair, and bent glasses. I noticed how easily they interacted with others, and how comfortable they were in their own skin. I wasn't introverted or shy; I was just embarrassed and ashamed. I couldn't be myself in their presence.

But I didn't stare *too* long. I couldn't afford for them to notice me. I couldn't impede on their beautiful aesthetic. I didn't want to make them uncomfortable. *They* were the type of girls who went to church summer camps with friends, not me. I just wanted to blend in. I'm glad Brittany was there with me. I used my childhood bff as my safety blanket. None of the rich girls spoke to me, and I was okay with that. It was better to go unacknowledged than to be seen for who I was. I kept my mouth shut and just smiled, hoping to make myself invisible. Hoping that I wasn't intruding on their special church camp experience.

I grew up in a predominantly white, conservative, well-resourced mega church in the Bible belt of Texas. I could articulate the gospel from the time I was about six years old. I had scriptures memorized, and all my peers did too. I was particularly excited about going to church camp, because all of the other cool girls my age had already been before. They raved about the memories they made at camp, year after year. My parents had always wanted me to go, but they were clear about how much of a stretch the cost of the camp was. This year, they saved up enough money for me to go. Before arriving, I was over the moon about my first week-long church camp experience.

Even though I didn't fit in, I thought to myself, "at least I can have God." I decided that I would make the most out of my time there. I spent mornings in quiet time outdoors with God. I read scripture, prayed, and basked in the apricot sunrise and the crisp, grassy air. Although I spent my childhood memorizing scripture, this was the first time I read the Bible to simply understand God. I sensed a nearness to God that was often fleeting. During a particular service that week, the call to salvation was given after the gospel was shared. Having grown up in church, I had prayed the prayer of salvation many times, but I wasn't confident that I would make it into heaven. That night, I prayed a different prayer.

"Lord, I accept you into my heart as my Lord and Savior. Thank you for forgiving me from my sin...." I began, reciting the prayer on auto-pilot.

"God, I don't know if I'm really saved. I want to be sure," I pivoted.

"I want a real relationship with you. I'm afraid of getting it wrong. I know I don't read my Bible enough, or pray enough, but I really do love you. I just want to know that I'm yours, and that I don't have to keep praying this prayer over and over. God, can you give me a sign? Can you give me like, a BIG sign?" I pleaded.

"God, I need confirmation. Please let me know either way. If I'm not saved, let me know. I'll change. If I am saved, let me know, and I'll live my whole life for you. I just need to know. So God, please send me a sign by the end of church camp. I just want to be right by you." I ended. I desperately sought God's acceptance and approval.

The next day during free time, I found myself chatting with some kids by a swing set. It felt good to branch out from my safety blanket—Brittany—and connect with some other kids my age. I stood under the hot sun. I sweat as the melanin in my skin absorbed the rays, tanning me to a toasty orange. After waiting my turn while others enjoyed the swingset on the hot summer day, I was eager to join. I hopped on a swing.

I began to swing back and forth, back and forth, back and forth. I felt the breeze through my frizzy hair as my curly ponytail bounced in sync with the pendulum. I laughed, lugging my weight around carelessly. I was having a blast. I swung even harder. I pointed my feet out. I swung even higher. I leaned back further. I felt compelled to test my own boundaries. I *knew* that I could swing higher than I ever had before. On the backswing of one enormous thrust of momentum, I cocked my whole body back and—

THUD!

I flipped backward. My body slammed the ground. I felt the weight of my body collide with the rocky gravel. It felt as if the blow to my back catapulted my lungs out of my body. I looked around in panic.

I couldn't breathe.

I opened my mouth to suck in air.

. . . nothing.

Over thirty seconds pass without air.

I was frozen in fear. I tried to search for air, but I couldn't find a sip. A blonde girl ran to help. She towered over me with a concerned face. "Are you okay?" She shrieked.

Over a minute without air had passed. I signaled to her that I couldn't breathe. I squirm and panic, laying flat on my back. It felt like I was suffocating. I thought I was dying. I prayed to God to spare me.

Suddenly, I gasped.

I steadied my breaths as the girl pulled me to my feet. I sat on a log to recoup. As I took time to process what happened, all of the pain of the fall came rushing to my body.

Most of the pain rushed to my ring finger on my right hand. I looked to see what was causing the pain. I had a bloody gash on my finger. The blood trailed from my finger down my hand. Wincing, I sent the blonde girl to ask for tissue and a band aid.

I sat by myself and examined the cut. I dabbed it dry with a tissue that the girl brought back to me. When I looked at the dried cut, the atmosphere shifted. I couldn't believe my eyes. My finger had been chiseled with the shape of a *check mark*. I couldn't stop staring at it. When blood rushed back to the cut, I would dab it again to reveal the check mark. I studied it. Could it be that this check mark on my finger was the sign that I was looking for? I had *just* asked God for confirmation in my salvation. I didn't want to be superstitious or weird, but I couldn't deny the uncanny feeling that God was trying to talk to me.

"Just *think* about it," I told myself. "You asked for a sign. God got your attention. He stopped you dead in your tracks. You'll never forget the time that you got the wind knocked out of you at church camp. He literally took your breath away. Then your finger got cut in the shape of a check mark—*equally unforgettable.* He allowed your flesh to be cut, and marked your body. This wasn't something that will easily go away. You'll constantly feel the throbbing in your finger and remember it."

I believed that the blow to my body and the blood I shed was symbolic of His body that was broken and His blood that was shed for me. The check mark looked to me like God's own stamp of approval. At the time, I remembered learning that the mark of the beast—the symbol that would separate those who belonged to the world and those who belonged to God—would be a sign in the last days. I remembered learning that the mark, likely 666, would either be found on your forehead or on your *right hand* (Rev. 13:16). The fact that *my* right hand had been branded by God shook me to the core. I concluded that while others would choose the mark of the beast, I had already been stamped with the mark of God. I belonged to Him. It felt like our insider secret.

I sat all alone on a tree stump, staring at my finger. I burst out in tears, smiling and thanking God. If God would go to such lengths to show me that I belonged to Him, then my fall was a cause for celebration! I cried happy tears, responding with praise and gratitude to God. I knew that I was chosen. I knew that I was set apart. I knew that He sent me the sign that I had begged for, and He sent it in a way that I understood and received. I vowed that I would serve Him with my whole life, because He chose to validate me.

The following night, we had a church service. I don't remember what was talked about, but I do remember worship. The lights were low and the speakers were booming. I got lost in the energy of the room. I stopped caring about who noticed me or not. I freely lifted my hands in the back of a room filled with over 300 other middle schoolers. With my arms lifted high, my ring finger on my right hand continued to throb. It was cause to lift my hands even higher. When I sang out to God, I focused so intently on the words I was singing. I sang to the God who chose me. I worshipped the God who validated me. It felt so intimate — like a passionate serenade. I felt on fire for God. I felt known. I knew that He was there with me in that room. He noticed me. He saw me. He valued me. He was the God who chose me and put the check mark on my finger. I didn't care if anyone else saw me, because I wasn't there for anyone else. I just wanted God, and anything else He had to offer me.

At the end of service, we were told that counselors were available to pray for us if we needed special prayer. For the first time, I decided to speak to an adult about my decision to give my life to God. I was nervous to tell her. What would she think? Would she tell me that my "sign" was invalid? Would she tell me that it's unbiblical? Would she write off what I believed to be confirmation from God as coincidental or unrelated? I took the risk and told her anyway.

"I know it may sound weird, but two days ago, I prayed for salvation." I began. "Then, I asked God to send me a sign to confirm that I really am saved. I wanted to know *for sure* that I'm going to heaven. Then, the next day, I fell off of a swing and cut my finger. I believe God used that to get my attention. When I looked at my finger, it was cut in the shape of a check mark. I believe that He is telling me that I'm saved and that I'm sealed for heaven. This was the sign that I was looking for." The words sounded a little weird coming out of my mouth, but it felt relieving to speak my truth.

She welcomed me with warmth and understanding. She asked me a few questions and listened to me. Soon after, she offered to pray for me. "God, thank you for the check mark that you left on Amanda's finger. Thank you that you've showed her that she is saved and that she belongs to You."

I was comforted by her prayer. She didn't judge me. She didn't dismiss my experience. She affirmed it in prayer before God. Suddenly, church camp was no longer about how dismissed, uncool or invisible I felt by the rich popular girls; it became about how loved, chosen and accepted I was by the Almighty God. I was sealed. I was seen. I was saved.

For over two years following church camp that summer, my finger was scarred. The scar was perfectly healed in the shape of a perfect check mark. Every time that I questioned God, I looked at my finger. Every time that I lacked faith, I looked at my finger. During times of disbelief, I looked at my finger. For years, it was a reminder that I was His.

YOU ARE CHOSEN

When we look for acceptance by our peers, one of two things happen: *One*, we will fall short of being accepted. *Two*, we'll be accepted only to realize that the acceptance falls short. Either way, it leaves us dry. Acceptance by others cannot fill the void in your heart. Only acceptance by God can. The validation that we search for in the world is readily available to us by way of Jesus Christ. God happily validates us. In fact, God *wants* to show us what we mean to Him.

The Bible makes this concept plain to us in Ephesians 1:4:

> *Even before he made the world, God loved us and chose us in Christ to be holy and without fault in his eyes. God decided in advance to adopt us into his own family by bringing us to himself through Jesus Christ. This is what he wanted to do, and it gave him great pleasure. So we praise God for the glorious grace he has poured out on us who belong to his dear Son. He is so rich in kindness and grace that he purchased our freedom with the blood of his Son and forgave our*

sins. He has showered his kindness on us, along with all wisdom and understanding.

This scripture puts it this way: God brings you to Him. God doesn't love the way that humans do. You don't have to wear the right thing, say the right thing, or even do the right thing before God loves you. He loved you first. You don't have to earn validation from God. He lavished His glorious grace over you through the sacrifice and resurrection of Jesus Christ on the cross because He *wanted* to!

God chose you before you could choose Him. God loved you before you could love Him. God isn't like the people who rejected you. God isn't like the people who ignored you. He sees you. He calls you. He makes Himself known to you. He's ready to shower you with His kindness, grace, and understanding. He's eager to see you as holy and without fault. He decided in advance to draw you to Him. Understand that the moment that you decide to surrender your life and your will for God's plan and will, you're accepted, graced, validated, and adopted.

There is no measure of validation on earth that could ever amount to the safety and satisfaction of being loved and chosen by God. Before we do anything for God, we are chosen. Before we change for God, we belong. Before we ever loved God, He first loved us. Without salvation, when you reach the end of yourself, you're empty and void. But when you're saved, when you reach the end of yourself, there you find God. God doesn't just tell you to get yourself together in order to be accepted. He comes to you, invites you to His table, and then gives you the Power to become more like Him.

When I arrived to church camp, I was met with feelings of shame, inferiority, and unworthiness by my peers. I was the outsider; I clung tightly to this identity throughout my life. Contrasting my feelings of rejection was God's acceptance. He embraced me with feelings of approval, importance, and dignity.

Stop right now and ask yourself, "Do I have a relationship with God the Father? Have I confessed my sin to Jesus for Him to cover and cleanse? Have I given the Holy

Spirit room to change me? If I died today, would I know that I'm truly saved for all of eternity?"

If the answer to any of these questions is *no*, then you have a decision to make right now. Life will fall short if you live it for yourself. The acceptance from people won't fulfill you. The validation from others won't fulfill you. You'll never feel known without intimacy with God. You'll never feel safe without eternal security. You'll never feel empowered without the Holy Spirit. You'll never feel free without the blood of Jesus. If you're ready to finally *belong*, then make the decision today to submit your life to God.

First, confess out loud in prayer that you have been running your life on your own and that you need God's leadership. Confess that you're a sinner and that you need the sacrifice of Jesus to restore you to right standing with God. Then, ask for the Holy Spirit to come into your heart to empower you to grow, change, and rewrite your story for good. Lastly, commit to yourself that you'll no longer live your life for yourself, but you'll live your life for the glory of God.

After you've done this, you need to tell another Christian that you have made a commitment to live for God. Much like how I did with the camp counselor at church camp, partner with someone in truth. Let someone else know that you've made a decision and a commitment to God. This is the first step of your new life that's no longer weakened by your imperfection, but instead empowered by God's perfection.

If you've already been saved, then take this opportunity to ask God for a renewed understanding of your identity as His daughter and your power through the Spirit of God. Make a commitment that you'll stop listening to the voice of the enemy and you'll choose to believe the Truth; that you'll allow the Bible to renew the way that you see yourself, think about yourself, and conduct yourself (Romans 12:2).

Moving forward, you belong. You are the daughter of the Most-High God. You are co-heirs with Christ. You are choice vessel for the Holy Spirit. You are not an outsider; you are deeply known. There is no rejection; there is only God's protection. God poured out forgiveness on you. He forgot all of your mistakes. You'll no longer seek for acceptance from people, worldly success, control over your own life, or perfection by your own standards. You'll delight in His love. You won't strive to earn His love, but you'll rest easily in the depths of His grace.

THIS WASN'T A COINCIDENCE

"Do you guys believe in fate and destiny, or do you think that things just happen by coincidence?" Justin said to the group as we walked across a busy street, making our way to a college party.

I wrestled with the question. If everything happened because of fate and destiny, then I had every right to be bitter. I rejected the thought, shaking it well out of my head. I looked to Rob on the other side of me to see if he had a perspective. He kept walking and listening.

"Like, the fact that we're all here together right now. Are our paths supposed to cross? Is it just a random coincidence that we're around each other tonight, or do you think that everything happens for a reason?" Justin asked again.

This was my first time ever having a real conversation with Justin. I saw him around school. We had lots of mutual connects. He was one well-known around campus. Having spent my freshman year cooped up and depressed in my dorm room, I decided that sophomore year would be different. So, tonight was an opportunity for me to tread the waters of social interaction. *Don't screw this up,* I coached myself.

But... I was flustered by the question. Isn't he supposed to be talking about girls, drinks, and the latest Kendrick Lamar album? Why was Justin being so deep right now? First of all, I don't know him. Second of all, I'm not trying to find a deeper meaning in life on my way to knocking back shots.

I couldn't help it. "No, I don't think that everything happens for a reason. I think that many things could just be a coincidence." I said.

I didn't really believe it, but I said it. I felt the tension of the lie inside of me. Rob felt my discomfort. I noted his laid-back posture shifting as he felt my energy. This felt touchy, but it wasn't supposed to. Rob's body language directed me to chill. He was my best friend at the time, and he read me like a book.

Justin looked at me funny. "So you're telling me that you think everything is just some random coincidence and that there's no meaning in any of this?"

"Some things are choices. Some things just *happen*. There isn't *always* a deeper meaning to things." I responded.

"Why do you say that?" He prodded.

"I don't know, I just don't think so." I answered, feeling uncomfortably seen.

Justin raised his eyebrow. "So the fact that in this moment, we're all together and our paths crossed... you don't think that the timing, place, or anything is interconnected or meant to be?"

"I mean, maybe. Not everything is a coincidence. But most everything is." I said.

I sounded dumb. I *knew* my argument sucked. I felt vapid and evasive. The question just blindsided me. So many wonders were swirling around in my head as resentment was tightening in my gut. Why was he bringing this up right now? Why does it feel like I'm flopping the conversation around like a clumsy person with a bar of slippery soap? Why am I ruining a perfectly-beautiful philosophical talk with my cynicism and skepticism?

Had Justin seen me sitting in on the back row of services at the campus ministry in the Student Center, crying because I don't believe that God loves me? Does he know that I'm rejecting religion and joined the mailing list for the secular humanists club? Why am I lying to myself? Why am I lying to Justin? . . . and why is he looking at me like that?

"What do you think, Robbie?" I redirected.

"I believe in fate," he said, shrugging his shoulders.

Great, I thought to myself. *Thanks for the help, Rob.*

I just wanted to do something social, and my first conversation with Justin was dismissive, vapid, and all-over-the-place. I assumed we'd wade in the shallow waters of small talk, but he decided to take a plunge in the deep end; I could barely swim. Having been running from God, I felt exposed. Wanting to reject the depths of spirituality and fate to explore the world of meaninglessness, why did it seem like God wouldn't *just leave me alone?*

I was going to this party to escape God, escape my pain, and escape myself, but Justin's questions forced me to confront the commitments that I once professed in worship to God, the "signs" that I knew God once showed me, the supernatural dreams that I couldn't explain away, and everything else having to do with all that I wanted to distance myself from. I wasn't searching for God or meaning like Justin was. I *knew* God, but I was running away.

All I wanted to do was make a good first impression, relax and *blend in*. I just *always* seemed to put my foot in my mouth around the cool crowd. After being raised in church to be equipped to initiate conversations about God, who would have thunk that I would fumble this conversation? No matter where I went—the church or the world—I didn't fit in. I stuck out like a sore thumb.

Heading nowhere fast, Justin eventually gave up on me and changed conversations. I walked the rest of the way not saying much, as to not ruin the vibes any more with my piecy, spacey arguments. I just wanted to forget that one of my deepest fears was playing out: that I would never be palatable to those who I wanted acceptance from; that I would always feel socially awkward and I would never know the right things to do or say; and that neither the church nor the world had a place for me to belong.

I just wanted to escape. I needed a *drink*.

Whenever I wasn't left alone to my own thoughts, the party was fun. I masked my feelings with spiked punch and a fake smile. I danced with a tall, happy guy. Cheered on some people playing beer pong. Chatted with some sorority girls. Spent time in the bathroom drunkenly critiquing my body. Left the bathroom trying to forget. Drank some more. I found Robbie and used his social cred to introduce me to new people. I watched people dance and laugh. I danced and laughed a few times myself. I drank some more.

After that night, I staggered back drunk with Robbie to his dorm room. His place was our spot to crash. His room welcomed me with the smell of Polo Black cologne, engineering textbooks, and semi-clean laundry. Having spent most of my sophomore year with my dread-headed best friend, this smell had become my comfort. We sat outside of his room to talk, giving his roommate a chance to sleep.

My world was spinning, but I definitely hadn't drank enough. Not enough to stop the negative voices in my head. I slid down the wall, crouching to a plop. I supported my head with my hand, looking down as tears started to well up in my eyes. I let the warm tears trail down my face.

My thoughts taunted, "You don't fit in. People don't like you. Remember that conversation with Justin? Yeah, you screwed that one up. You don't say the right things. You're too flippant when people are serious, but you're too uptight when people are having fun. You can't get it right. You're an imposter."

"What's going on?" Robbie said, unaware of the internal battle I was losing.

"Nothing," I said, too prideful to admit my seemingly-trivial insecurities.

"Why are you crying?" Robbie asked gently, as a good friend should.

Sniff. I had too much of a buzz to keep it all inside. I just let go. With streams running down my face, I complain, "Why does it feel like I never fit in?!"

Robbie didn't seem empathetic anymore. He seemed annoyed. He looked around with a frustrated sigh, his swinging dreadlocks accenting his every move.

"What?!" I asked defensively, snapping out of my drunken sob.

He shook his head. "Nothing."

It didn't sound like *nothing*. Now I was becoming frustrated.

27

"What is it? Why do you seem upset?" I slurred.

Sigh.

. . .

". . . You wanna know why I think you don't fit in?"

"Why?" I asked, desperate.

He turned his head one last time, looking around. The anticipation was killing me. I couldn't stand his grandiose pauses, especially right now. I remembered that he was drunker than I was. It always made him more dramatic. When he turned his face to look back at me, he seemed different. He seemed stable, sure, and sober; almost authoritative. When he opened his mouth, his voice sounded different, too.

"Because I believe God has a plan for your life."

I was stunned. I wasn't expecting that. Not from him. Not right now.

I was speechless...

I had to catch my breath.

Robbie didn't look like that. Robbie didn't sound like that. Robbie couldn't have thought that up on an average day, let alone while drunk after a long, partied-out night. Plus, it was *exactly* what I needed to hear. The entire night, I had been running from God all while God was chasing me down. This was His opportunity to finally grab my attention. In that moment, I knew beyond the shadow of a doubt that I had heard the voice of God.

Although I grew up in church, this was an unfamiliar message. The Christian life was about what I could do for God, but never what God would do for my future. I never heard talk about purpose. I never heard talk about a plan. To me, the Christian life was about living differently than the world by doing the right thing. I had to figure it out on my own; I didn't think that God would deliberately lay out a path for my life.

Suddenly, my frustrations made sense. The voice of truth dispelled every lie. Of *course* I couldn't fit in with people who didn't know God—I wasn't called to be influenced by them; I was called to influence them. My life had value, purpose, and intention. God cared so much about me that He Himself wouldn't allow me to choose the wrong path. He knew that I couldn't afford to be out of alignment with His perfect plan. As long as I was running from God, hoping for approval and acceptance, then I would never recognize my true identity.

GOD HAS A PLAN FOR YOUR LIFE

Fitting in is a losing battle when you're marked by God. The Apostle Paul in the book of Galatians explains it this way: "Am I trying to please people? If I were still trying to please people, I would not be a servant of Christ." I would take this verse a step further and assert that people-pleasing is a form of idolatry. That night, I was idolizing the opinions of people. I sought to please them. And, who you seek to please becomes the God of your life. If you work to please God, then you prove your identity as both a servant and daughter of God. However, if you strive to please people, then you belittle your God-identity.

I had been running from God, hoping to abandon my identity. I felt as if God had failed me. My life was marked by pain. I no longer wanted to be identified by the God who seemed to "let" horrible things—fatherhood rejection, rape and cheating by a boyfriend, falling into depression and suicidal thoughts—happen to me. I couldn't make sense of how a loving God could let my soul rot in my pain. Little did I know that no matter how far I ran, I took my identity with me. I couldn't erase the mark of God. I couldn't emancipate myself as a daughter of God. No matter how much I drank, I couldn't escape His plan. He was the one who was calling me that night. He was the one who pursued me, grabbing my attention twice in one night. He never let me out of His sight.

Even when you lose sight of your identity, God doesn't lose sight of you. He loves you too much to abandon you. Many times, we attempt to forfeit our true identity as children of God because we're hurt. It is easy to allow your pain to shape your view of God, instead of allowing God to shape your view of pain. When you try forfeit your identity as God's daughter, you look to the world to father you. You ask for people to define you. You put the power of your value and worth in the hands of fickle humans. You say to them, "define me!" when your creator is saying, "I already have!" You surrender your God-authority to people who don't even know Him.

In short, if you've submitted your life to Christ—if you've prayed the prayer of salvation—then your new identity is *child of God*. When you belong to God, you can't find the satisfaction of approval from others. Their approval is a cheap substitute for the real thing. Let's look at what scripture says about our identity: "See how very much our Father loves us, for he calls us his children, and that is what we are! But the people who belong to this world don't recognize that we are God's children because they don't know him" (1 John 3:1-3). This scripture presents that those in the world don't know God and therefore won't comprehend the God in you. You'll strive and strive for their approval, only for the reward of rejection.

The tension is there because unbelievers don't have the same father that you do! Their father is the devil (John 8:44). They don't share your DNA and they won't speak your language. You speak the language of heaven, and they speak the language of hell. Even if you learn their language and speak their language, they will hear your accent. You can be fluent in hell, but someone will inevitably say, "You sound funny. You're not from around here."

You're a daughter of the highest God! You belong to the Kingdom of Heaven! Stop playing small when you were made to be big. You didn't belong to those people, anyway! You belong to God. You live for an audience of ONE. If you please unbelievers, then you're really just making their demons smile. Why would you want applause and approval from people that the enemy applauds and approves of? Your job is to pull them out of darkness, not succumb to it. No matter how hard you'll try to dim your light, the Holy Spirit is too bright. Demons recognize the Holy Spirit, even if you're trying to conceal Him. God will NOT be compromised.

If you're a child of God but you haven't been living like one, then God is going to go to great lengths to get your attention. He will allow you to experience the tension, dissonance and frustration of being a square peg in a round hole. Discomfort in the world is there to push you towards comfort in God. God doesn't want you to feel comfortable being someone you're not. He'll let you feel rejected. He'll allow you to feel different. He'll allow you to feel lonely. Why? Because God's love is better than anything the world has to offer. The feeling of loneliness is an invitation for *intimacy* with God. God wants to give you more. He knows that if He can get alone with you, you'll experience His abundant love and grace. He'll speak identity over you. He'll reveal His plan for you.

My son will do things just like me. My husband likes to make fun of me and say, "you act just like Bean!" The truth is that Elijah (aka Bean) acts just like me. Why? Because he's my son. He has my DNA. Even if he goes to great lengths to change his behavior, he still looks like me; he still bears my last name. I birthed him. No matter where he goes in life, that will never change his identity as my son.

This concept holds true when we're born again. Through God, we are birthed into a new spiritual family. We have God's spiritual DNA—the Holy Spirit. The Holy Spirit changes us, making us more like God. No matter where we go, how far we stray, the Holy Spirit bears our identity.

You may think "a little compromise is fine," but the Holy Spirit inside of you—the one who confirms your God-identity—will tell you otherwise. You'll feel two-faced when you post a promiscuous photo. You'll feel deceitful when you join in the gossip. You'll feel like a fraud when you are in a sin-filled environment.

Even others will be surprised when they see you behaving in a way that contradicts your identity. They'll say, "it's confusing seeing you post something like that. I thought you were *different*." Or, "what are *you* doing hanging out in a place like this?" Everyone sees it, even if you want to deny it. You are filled with the Holy Spirit. You are of royal blood. You are an image-bearer of God.

Do you need a reminder of who you are? Are you like how I was after that night of partying, sulking over the hopelessness of the world; realizing that it will always leave you dry? Maybe you're saved and Spirit-filled, but you've been seeking the approval of people. Maybe you've lacked a sense of identity, so you've been looking outside of yourself to find it. Maybe you've never heard anyone speak purpose or identity over your life. Maybe you don't feel loved by God, cherished by God, or chosen by God. Maybe you just feel like you don't *belong*.

I want to tell you this:

God has a plan for your life. You are a child of God. You carry His DNA. There is nothing you can do to outrun His love. There is nothing you can do to earn His acceptance. You are not made to fit in. You are made to stand out. God accepts you. God is beside to you. God sees you. He hears you. He feels what you feel. You are known. You are loved. You belong. Assume your authority. Stand in your identity.

BELONG ACTION PLAN

What is inside of an egg is defined by the creature that lays the egg. If an ostrich lays an egg, then its egg is destined to become an ostrich. If a chicken lays an egg, then its egg is destined to become a chicken. When a butterfly lays an egg, then its egg is destined to become a butterfly. Before the antenna forms and before the wings take shape, the creature inside the egg has the DNA—the destiny—to be a butterfly. Before it proves itself by morphing into a butterfly, the egg is already identified by the one who laid it. Laying an egg is the work of the parent, *not* the offspring.

In that same way, when you are a child of God, God the Father lays your egg. You're born again. You don't have the power to lay your own egg; only your heavenly Father does. In the same way that a baby can't control its own birth, your new life is not something you work for or earn; your new life is a *gift*. Ephesians 1:3 (TPT) explains it this way:

*Every spiritual blessing in the heavenly realm has already been lavished upon us as a **love gift** from our* *wonderful heavenly Father, the Father of our Lord Jesus—all because he sees us **wrapped into Christ**. This is why we celebrate him with all our hearts! And he chose us to be **his very own**, joining us to himself even before he laid the foundation of the universe! Because of his great love, he ordained us, so that we would be seen as **holy in his eyes with an unstained innocence**.*

I love how The Passion Translation explains that the Father sees us "wrapped" into Christ. This beautiful picture perfectly transfers into the analogy of the butterfly egg. Let me explain. **God is three persons:** God the *Father*, God the Son (*Jesus*), and God the *Holy Spirit*. **God the Father** is like the butterfly that lays the egg. Because He chose to, He laid the egg, giving you new life and belonging as His daughter. He did so by laying down Jesus to die for the payment of your sins. **Jesus** (God the son) symbolizes the egg that wraps around you. When God sees you, He sees you "wrapped" in the egg, *wrapped* in the cleansing sacrifice and love of Jesus Christ.

40

Because you've just been born, you don't have the capacity to do anything for God. Your good works don't identify you. It's **Jesus' sacrifice** that identifies you as **God's daughter**. When He looks at you, God doesn't see your faults, shortcomings, and sins; as the scripture puts it, He sees you as "holy in his eyes with an unstained innocence." In short, the Father sees you wrapped into Jesus. He sees you as pure like Jesus is pure. He sees you as holy like Jesus is holy. He sees you as His child like Jesus is His child.

If **God the Father** is the butterfly that lays your new life, and **God the Son (Jesus)** is the egg that surrounds you and identifies you, then where does **God the Holy Spirit** fit into this picture? Let's keep digging into this passage of Ephesians to find out. The scripture continues in Verse 13b (NIV):

And you also were included in Christ when you heard the message of truth, the gospel of your salvation. When you believed, you were marked in him with a seal, the promised Holy Spirit, who is a deposit guaranteeing our inheritance until the redemption of

those who are God's possession—to the praise of his
glory.

It's telling us that once you're born again, God deposits **the Holy Spirit** into you. A deposit is the action of placing something in a specified place. The Holy Spirit is placed inside you like DNA inside of an egg, guaranteeing what the creature will become from the moment of its conception. Before you look like a Christian, stop doing sinful things, and have it all together, you're sealed with the DNA to empower you with the ability to mature and change. The good news is that while you're given the power to change, you're loved and accepted even before you do.

God isn't like the cool guys or the popular girls who seem to require a version of yourself before you're good enough to belong. God isn't like your earthly father, who may have rejected you when you fell short of his expectations. You don't have to audition for your place or perform your way into love. No—before you do anything flashy or glamorous for God, you **belong**. God the Father chose you, giving you new life through the sacrifice of Jesus, and empowered you to change with the deposit of the Holy Spirit. Even if you don't feel good enough, you are. Even though you see your disqualifiers, insecurities, and shortcomings, God sees you as His pure and holy daughter, wrapped into Jesus and empowered by the Holy Spirit.

LAY THE FOUNDATION

The first stage in the Life Cycle of Change is **Belong**. This stage is all about how you relate to God. I went through the *Belong* stage soon after Robbie told me that God had a plan for my life. On another occasion after that night, I stubbornly told Robbie, "I don't want to go to church just because others want me to. I don't want to feel pressured to go. I don't want to be fake."

"Then don't," Robbie said.

I was so shocked. I thought that Robbie was going to tell me how important church is, not that I should skip it.

"What do you mean?" I asked.

"If you don't want to go to church, then don't. Just *pray* and *read your Bible*."

This was another defining moment within my Life Cycle of Change. While I would eventually find a church home to belong to, I needed to stop worrying about belonging to others and focus on belonging to God. I understood that an authentic relationship with God was not built by the desire to even fit in with church folk; an authentic relationship with

45

God was built by doing something simple—praying and reading the Bible. After that day, I began reading the Bible on my own. The words would jump out to me, convict me, and breathe life into me. It was as if God was speaking directly to me. I also began praying. I started to talk to God, asking Him for direction, wisdom, and healing. In a matter of weeks, my hardened heart began to soften, my mindset began to shift, and my actions began to change.

Suddenly, I had the joy and the peace that I had been longing for. I didn't walk around with a chip on my shoulder; in fact, I felt lighter than I ever had before. I stopped calling myself an "agnostic" and researching other religions. I stopped having emotional breakdowns and suicidal thoughts. I felt like I could breathe again. I saw the world with fresh eyes again. I started having weekly Bible studies with a friend of mine who didn't judge me before I had it "all together." I didn't look to those Bible studies like a burden. I actually I looked forward to those Bible studies like they were an escape from the worries and weights of life.

After a couple months of praying, reading the Bible, and cultivating my relationship with God the Father, I desired to go to church. After visiting a few places, I found a church home to belong to. I understood that I belonged to God before I belonged to the church. Understanding that freed me from going to church in order to validated by church people; instead, I went to church because I was ready to take the next step in my relationship with God. Simply because I was compelled to, I stopped cursing and getting drunk. To my surprise, it wasn't hard to give up. All I wanted to do was to make my Father happy. I belonged to Him, and not the world.

If you are in the *Belong* stage of The Life Cycle of Change, understand that external pressures and expectations will not change you. Whether you're faking the funk in church or faking the funk with the world in order to find acceptance and validation, know that you'll never feel yourself without understanding who you are. **You belong to God**. He desires to know you. He desires to speak to you. In order to mature in your identity, you must build an authentic relationship with God. Oftentimes, this part is tricky for Christians. For some reason, it can be easier to play church by following a dress code, using churchy lingo and having deep revelatory knowledge to share, rather than actually spending time with God. God is much less concerned with how well you can preach and teach, and is much more concerned with your intimacy with Him. Matthew 7:21-23 explains this concept best:

> Not everyone who says to me, 'Lord, Lord,' will enter the kingdom of heaven, but the one who does the will of my Father who is in heaven. On that day many will say to me, 'Lord, Lord, did we not prophesy in your name, and cast out demons in your name, and do many mighty works in your name?' And then will I declare to them, 'I never knew you; depart from me, you workers of lawlessness. '

Do you know that there are many people on earth that appear to be super-spiritual, yet God doesn't even know them? Does it surprise you can be gifted to do the work of God, yet still be headed straight toward hell? That's because God could care less about your ability to exorcise a demon if you don't even talk to Him all of the other hours of the day. God cares more about your time with Him than the talents that you use for Him. He's more concerned with your focused attention than your flashy abilities. Simply put, God wants YOU.

This scripture shouldn't scare you; it should refresh you. It's reminding you that salvation isn't about how great you can be all by yourself; salvation is simply built upon you knowing God and God knowing you. Your ticket into heaven isn't a scale that weighs your good deeds against your bad deeds. Your ticket into heaven isn't even a secret passcode that only the spiritual elite know. No—your only way into heaven is through relationship with God that is established upon the sacrifice of Jesus Christ.

Think about it this way: why would God force you to spend the rest of eternity with Him if you never wanted to spend any time on earth with Him? God is beckoning you to choose to build a true, life-giving relationship with Him. And God doesn't just want the relationship for Himself; God wants the relationship for *you*. Let's be honest, living for God is hard! He knows how hard it is, so God simply doesn't want you to do it alone. Righteous living was never meant to be done without relational living. God knows that you can't be fully dedicated to Him without drawing from Him. He knows that if you give your life to holiness but you never drink from the well of His love, joy, and peace-filled presence, then you're going to burn out and resent that you ever became a Christian in the first place. You efforts for God should never outweigh your intimacy with God. If you're ready to build a genuine relationship with God, it begins with cultivating a prayer life and reading the Bible.

CULTIVATING A PRAYER LIFE

BECOMING A FRIEND OF GOD

Do you talk to God every day? Does God feel like a genie that you call on wishfully whenever you need help, or does God feel like your Father who you know intimately? Prayer isn't something that we should access whenever we have a need. Prayer also isn't something that you just block off in the beginning of your day for a set period of time. Prayer is an ongoing conversation that you have with God throughout the day in every situation. Rather than thinking of prayer to God as one 5-minute phone call you have every morning, later to forget about God, think of prayer as an ongoing text message conversation with your best friend. Your "amen" is how you press "send." Some messages are long, and some messages are short. It goes back and forth like a ping-pong match. You text throughout the day. You ask a question, and you wait for a response. You share your highs and you share your lows. The conversation thread never ends.

Prayer is just that—an ongoing conversation. 1 Thessalonians 5:16-18 says, "Always be joyful. Never stop praying. Be thankful in all circumstances, for this is God's will for you who belong to Christ Jesus." Prayer isn't something that was ever made to crossed off of your to-do list. This is simply because it's never done. Prayer is open-ended, open-forum, and open-invite. Don't wait for something good to happen to thank God. Don't wait for something bad to happen to talk to God. Don't wait for anything to happen in order for you to open yourself to communicate with your creator.

Prayer is a privilege. We don't have to pray, we *get* to pray. We are blessed to know the God who laid the foundations of the earth. The One who set the planets into motion wants to address your pains. The God who orchestrates the universe laughs and cries with you. If God never did anything else for us, He sent Jesus to die for us; yet, still He wants to know us, surround us, and walk with us. Hebrews 4:15-16 says,

> *For we do not have a high priest who is unable to empathize with our weaknesses, but we have one who has been tempted in every way, just as we are—yet he*

did not sin. Let us then approach God's throne of grace with confidence, so that we may receive mercy and find grace to help us in our time of need.

We know God to be the King of Kings and the Lord of Lords, yet He empathizes with our thoughts and feelings, victories and struggles. This is because God made Himself human through His son, Jesus Christ. When Jesus walked the earth, He lived the life that we should have lived—perfect and blameless. But just because He never sinned doesn't mean that He never struggled. He felt every temptation that we feel, and endured. Because of Jesus, God understands our pains and our joys. He lived it. This scripture in Hebrews is telling us that because we belong, we have the highest privilege to boldly and confidently communicate with God at *anytime*.

PRAYER IS A PRACTICE, NOT A PERFORMANCE

We've all heard a prayer rambler before... They'll say the same thing over and over, just in different churchy ways. Their voice changes from their normal speech, and it suddenly becomes more articulated, punctuated and and fluctuated. They may alternate between the titles, "Lord God," "Father God," too many times to count. Even though they're saying a lot of words, because they're working so hard to sound *deep*, you're not really sure what point they're actually making. Their prayer becomes distracting, because rather than focusing on God, you're distracted by them. Whether you're guilty of being a prayer rambler, or someone you know is a prayer rambler, know that it's not supposed to be that way.

The Bible talks about what happens when prayer ceases to be a conversation between you and God and starts to become a performance. Matthew 6:5-15 says,

And when you pray, do not be like the hypocrites, for they love to pray standing in the synagogues and on the street corners to be seen by others. Truly I tell you, they have received their reward in full. But when you pray, go into your room, close the door and pray to your Father, who is unseen. Then your Father, who sees what is done in secret, will reward you. And when you pray, do not keep on babbling like pagans, for they

think they will be heard because of their many words.
Do not be like them, for your Father knows what you
need before you ask him.

Prayer is not a performance. Prayer isn't an opportunity for you to showcase how well you can speak, and it's not an opportunity to impress God. You shouldn't feel nervous whenever you pray in public, because it's not for anyone else to judge or critique. As a pastor's wife, I have had the privilege of leading prayer in front of my church. At times, I've worried about sounding compelling and not stumbling over my words. Because I hated that feeling, I decided that I needed to get good at delivering prayer. So, I started listening to compelling and clearly-articulated prayers, and began practicing and mimicking their style. After a while, I began to feel convicted. I knew that I was more focused on how I sounded than I was focused on God. Prayer isn't something that you have to practice in private so that you can stunt in public. No, rather than practicing prayer, make prayer your *practice*.

The word *practice* can be used as both a noun and a verb. When used as a verb, to practice means to "perform an activity or exercise a skill repeatedly or regularly in order to improve or maintain one's proficiency." This is NOT the mentality that we should adopt when it comes to prayer. We shouldn't chalk up some churchy, pretentious jargon in order to sound super-spiritual when we pray in public. Instead, we should make prayer our practice—the *noun*.

When used as a noun, a practice is, "the business of a professional person." When you hear someone say that they own a nursing practice, that means that that nursing is their business, taking up everyday space in their life. Nursing is their business—it's top of mind, always relevant, and where their focus is. When you treat prayer as your business, your *practice*, it is so ingrained in you that you do it out of habit. You create a culture of conversation between you and God, and you make a practice out of it; your business is always God's business. You're able to tug on the heartstrings of the heavens at any given moment because you're always in the presence of God. God knows you and you know God. Rather than living your life without leaving any space for God to speak, you welcome Him into every moment. You don't feel pressured to sound like anyone else, impress anyone else, or find the right words to say, because whenever you pray, you're simply continuing a conversation that you've been having. It's your way of life. Don't diminish prayer into a Sunday-morning performance; exalt prayer to an everyday practice.

HOW TO PRAY

Jesus actually modeled how we should pray. This is commonly known as "the Lord's Prayer." Instead of treating the Lord's prayer as a religious dogma to recite without thought, we can use it as a guide to begin our own authentic conversation with God. Let's break down each element of the Lord's prayer to learn how to begin a relationship with God:

Our Father in Heaven,	Connect with God relationally
hallowed be your name,	Worship His name
your kingdom come, your will be done, on earth as it is in heaven.	Pray His agenda first
Give us today our daily bread,	Depend on Him for everything
And forgive us our debts, as we also have forgiven our debtors.	Forgive and be forgiven
And lead us not into temptation, but deliver us from the evil one.	Engage in spiritual warfare
For yours is the kingdom and the power and the glory forever. Amen.	Express faith in God's ability

It's important to not treat the Lord's prayer like a rule book. Whether you pray all seven elements of the prayer each day, or you focus on one each day of the week, you're building. Use this chart as a tool to help you grow intimately closer to God. Whether you're driving in traffic, putting your kid to sleep, or completing an assignment at work, you can send God a quick message about connection with Him, worship of Him, reverence for His will, dependence on His hand, forgiveness for His people, spiritual warfare against the enemy, or faith in

His plan. Know that you belong to God and you can talk to Him anytime, anyplace, about anything.

HEARING GOD'S VOICE

Lastly, one key element of prayer is *listening*. How would you feel if you had a friend who always talked to you, but never listened to your response? They hogged the conversation, asked for help and advice, yet never stopped to leave room to receive your advice. You knew you could help them, if they would just *listen*. How would that make you feel? I know that my biggest pet peeve is when people make assumptions about me, what I think, and what I would say, yet never taking the time to ask and listen. I wonder if God feels the same way—often accessed, but hardly listened to, and misunderstood.

In order to hear God's voice, listen. One exercise that I practice and encourage others to practice is the "Hearing God's Voice" exercise. It's very simple.

- First, you envision either God the Father, Jesus, or the Holy Spirit standing in front of you. (They're all God, so simply choose one).

- Next, you'll ask Him a question that you'd like to know. (Ex. "Father, can you show me why this hurts me so much? Can you show me why I'm struggling to let go?")

- Then, you leave space and silence.

- Write down whatever you think, feel, notice, sense, imagine, envision, remember, and more. Sometimes God will place a song on your heart. He may even bring related scripture to mind. Other times, God may give you a *knowing* of what is true. Many times, God will guide your thoughts and open your eyes to the truth. There are no limits to the way that God communicates you.

Hearing God's voice is as simple as that! I've done this exercise with more women than I can count, and it is highly effective. I encourage you to use this strategy at least once a day. With time and consistency, you'll grow to become familiar with the way that God communicates with you. In John 10, Jesus teaches the Jews, "My sheep listen to my voice; I know them, and they follow me." If you don't confidently know God's voice, then continue to practice listening. You'll begin to trust that you're hearing Him, and not yourself. Over time, you'll be able to access His voice, His spirit and His wisdom at any given moment. You'll be able to say in the midst of a tough circumstance, "God, show me the truth about this scenario," or "God, what do you think about how I'm handling this dilemma?" You'll have the capacity to hear God's voice and follow it.

READING THE BIBLE

The Bible isn't like any other book. While all other books can offer you trending opinion and temporary knowledge, the Word of God tells you *truth*. Prose can give you momentary wisdom, a fleeting sense of adventure, or even a quick strategy. But the Bible is everlasting and never-ending. Its truths outlast this life. It is powerful and effective, standing the tests of time. The Word was with God in the beginning, and when all the world fades away, the Word will be there in the end.

While all other books are inanimate, the Word of God is awake. It was scripture that softened my hardened heart and breathed life into me. Hebrews 4:12 says, "For the word of God is alive and active. Sharper than any double-edged sword, it penetrates even to dividing soul and spirit, joints and marrow; it judges the thoughts and attitudes of the heart." Every other book we have the power to judge, but the Bible is the only book with the power to judge us. While you may not understand every passage, every historical nuance, or even every biblical name, keep reading. Even when it feels as if the Word is disrupting your comfort, continue to dig. The more you seek, the more you find. The more questions you ask, the more answers you get.

Have you already committed to a lifestyle of scripture study? If not, then now is the time to start. Don't allow intimidation to bark at you, making the task of this commitment seem too tall. Just take it a day at a time. **Take this time to set your alarm to go off every day at a set time**. If you don't have a plan or a physical devotional, use the Bible app and find a Bible plan to follow. The best places to start fresh are with the book of Proverbs and the book of John. Proverbs has 31 chapters, so it's an ideal book of the bible to read within a month, going through one chapter a day. The book of John gives you the entire story, start to finish, of Jesus' life on earth. This book is ideal if you need to learn or to be refreshed in who Jesus is, how He lived, and what He has done for you.

Commit to reading scripture every single day. Treat it like showering. Yesterday's shower won't hold you over for today. You need to be washed with the word every day. If you skip a day, your thoughts start to stink. If you skip two days, your feelings start to stink. If you skip a week, you're feel filthy all around, doing things you know you shouldn't be doing. You need the Word to wash you every single day. You can't just read it, but you must also apply it. James 1:22 says, "But don't just listen to God's word. You must do what it says. Otherwise, you are only fooling yourselves." Give God's Word the authority to correct you. Give the Bible room to change you. This is an essential foundation to our walk with Christ. This is a fundamental process for you to mature, grow, and change.

STAGE TWO
SHED

FALSE NARRATIVES

I inched toward the living room, hesitancy leading the way. I was wearing a new orange skirt; well, new-*ish*. It was a hand-me-down from a family friend. I didn't get clothes often, and when I did, they never had tags on them. In this case, I was eager to try on a style I had never worn before. The stretchy skirt wrapped around my midsection and covered the tops of my thighs, but it left a good five inches between its hem and my knee. I knew that before I left the house in it, the skirt had to make it past my dad. I approached my father, who was sitting on the couch. He took one look at me in disapproval.

"Where are you going in that skirt?" He asked, face scrunched up.

"I don't know," I said.

"Turn around," he commanded. He assessed the appropriateness of the skirt from all around. I began to shrink.

"You can't show all of that. You need to wear something that will cover your legs. Go back and change."

I looked down at my thighs, jiggly and thick. I assessed my stomach, round and wide. He was right. I couldn't show this body. I couldn't wear this skirt. I was overcome with shame and sadness. Shame, because I didn't have the body to wear what other girls wore; sadness, because I wanted to be pretty, and I wasn't.

I was about eight years old. This memory had been archived into the abyss of my mind, never to be accessed again. I have stored away so much of my childhood somewhere amongst the backlogged files too, and most of those memories are brief. It wasn't until I was asked to recall the first memory I had when I did not feel beautiful that I was able to retrieve such a fuzzy day. While the memory was blurry, it was a critical one. It was a defining moment for me. It was a day when my internal narrative was being written, later to be reinforced. This narrative said:

You're not pretty.

You don't fit in with the "cool girls."

If you were skinny, then you'd be accepted.

There's something wrong with your body.

You should be ashamed to be who you are.

You should hide who you are.

The narrative began there, but it didn't end there. I was programmed to believe that I could never lose weight, I could never be athletic, I could never have nice things, I could never be socially important, I could never be enough, and that I could never change.

This narrative followed me throughout my life, even into early adulthood. I felt inferior to the pretty, the skinny, the wealthy, and the popular. When I saw other girls, I saw what they had, and inevitably what I had not. This belief of being less-than was so deeply-rooted that it affected how I carry myself, how I spoke to myself, the friendships I did and didn't make, the guys I did and didn't date, the people I did and didn't talk to, the places I did and didn't visit, the things I did and didn't say, the clothes I did and didn't wear, and so much more. The seed of lack, inferiority, and self-doubt was planted while I was young. Then, that small seed sprouted into winding weeds that attempted to choke out the abundant harvest that God died to bear in my life.

Even after I surrendered my life to God for good, I wrestled between who I used to be and who I could be. I believed in God. I knew Jesus. I was saved. I wasn't held back because of sin. I wasn't stifled because of disobedience. The problem was not that I didn't believe in God; the problem was that I didn't believe in *myself*. Surrendering my life to God was the key that unlocked the cage of lack, inferiority, and self-doubt that held me captive throughout my life. But even after He unlocked it, I sat in that cage. I couldn't see life beyond it. Who was I without hating my body? What did I think about if I wasn't considering my lack? What would be required of me if I believed in myself? Who would I become if I could *choose*? How much is it going to cost me to change?

Saved but Stuck

Maybe you're like me. You've believed a story about who you are from a young age, and the story has stuck. You're exhausted by the feelings of inadequacy. You're plagued by the feelings of inferiority. You've broken free from much of who you "used to be," yet you still fear that who you used to be will resurface with a vengeance. You want to live for God,

72

but your frustration with how He created you weighs you down. You want to walk in purpose, but the plans that God has for you don't match the narratives that you've believed about yourself. You wonder if you could ever be different. You wonder if you could ever be more. You wonder if you could truly *change*.

Stage Two in the Life Cycle of Change is *Shed*. The Shed stage requires you to let go of all of the dead that doesn't serve you. This includes sin, shame, self-doubt, insecurity, limiting beliefs, false mentalities, faulty programming, and more. This stage also requires you to lay aside the dead weight of unforgiveness and embrace emotional healing. You don't have to be who you've always been. You don't have to be pushed around by societal standards, religious expectations, or even previous mentalities. You have permission to lay aside everything that no longer serves you so that you can take up what does. You'll stand firm in your Christ-identity so that you can discard your false identity.

WHAT'S THE NARRATIVE?

What is a false narrative that you've clung tightly to throughout your life? Maybe you always felt flawed and defective. Maybe you've always felt unlovable. It could be that you don't feel valuable or worthwhile without being the *best*. Maybe you have always worried that others have something that you don't have. Have you have always felt lonely, like no one else understands your inner-world? Maybe you fear that those around you will leave you when it matters most. Have you felt like others are trying to control you, and you're worried that you will never be free? Or maybe you've felt like your voice doesn't matter, like your feelings are often overridden.

These are some examples of narratives that follow us throughout our lives. Whenever you encounter anything that looks remotely like this narrative, the enemy will suggest that you're being abandoned again, rejected again, picked last again, misunderstood again, or whatever else. It could be that your friend has to focus more on her career than normal for a time, leaving less time for you. The enemy will suggest that she's going to stop needing you, and eventually move on.

Even though that's not true, it triggers you. You'll think, "here we go again. I knew this would happen." Because this narrative becomes something you expect, then it becomes a narrative that you project.

You stop believing that good could come your way. You assume the worst. You wait for things to fall apart. You prophesy that things can't work out for your good, because they never do. When someone speaks an encouraging word over you, you follow it up with sabotage. Your worst fears become your reality. It becomes a self-fulfilling prophecy. When God presents an opportunity for growth and change, you go back to the cycle and narrative that you've always known.

Have you ever said things like,

"those people never like me. I'll never fit in with them."

"I'm not good at doing that. That's simply not my thing."

"This never works out for me."

"All men are bad."

"Nothing is as good as it seems."

It could be that at one time, you did believe the best. You did hope for brighter days. You did trust in the goodness of people. You did work to improve. You tried the hard thing. You prayed the bold prayer. But when things didn't work out the way you thought they should, instead of asking God for understanding, you listened to the suggestion of the enemy. You let him remind you of the false narrative. He said things like,

"See, this is what happens when you hope. You'll always be disappointed."

"See, this is why you can't depend on anyone else."

"See, this is why you shouldn't speak up. Don't use your voice. Don't rock the boat."

"See, you can't be vulnerable with others. They always exploit you."

"See, you shouldn't step out on faith. You always fail anyway."

It seems easier to take hold of the false narrative than to ask God for clarity, redirection, and truth. When you grow accustomed to the way things have always been, whether or not those patterns and beliefs serve you, you feel bound to them. If you want to change your life and rewrite your narrative, then you *need* God. Knowing the Trinity — God in three persons — you'll have a revelation of who you are. You need the redemptive sacrifice of **Jesus** to free you from the confines of sin — past, present, and future. You need to be identified as a beloved daughter of **God the Father**. You also need the power of the **Holy Spirit** to preach the truth to you, empower you, and to change you from the inside out. I said it before and I'll say it again: when you don't have the Holy Spirit, who you are is all you'll ever be. But when you have the Holy Spirit, who you become is who you were meant to be.

FOUR-AM THERAPY SESSION

It was nearly four in the morning. I was tired. I was hungry. My eyes were burning. But. . . I didn't care. The conversation was just *too good*. We had been talking non-stop since 8pm. My two girlfriends and I were up chatting about the darkest bits of our past, uncovering the sins and struggles that God had freed us from. For over an hour, we had been sharing these experiences—something that I had never done before. For the longest, I had been in a place of leadership. I hadn't had the opportunity to be vulnerable around other women who wouldn't judge me for the experiences that I had been through. I was so used to being the "strong one." This felt *so good*.

One friend confessed that she was in a sexually abusive relationship with a college boyfriend. When she shared her story, my body clenched and my heart broke. Her story was hard to listen to. I winced at the thought of the demonic act of a ruthless, selfish man. How could someone bring themselves to violate someone else's body? Well, I knew how. Her story was so painful to listen to because it

79

sounded all too familiar. I was having flashbacks of an unfortunately resemblant episode.

I remembered the day that I was walking in a field, hand-in-hand with a high school boyfriend. As we walked in the field, my stomach turned with dread. This didn't feel right. Every time he took me to this spot, he expected something from me... something that I wasn't prepared to give. This field was filled with bad memories; memories of pressured kisses and unwanted touches. . . Pressure and coercion. Compromised boundaries. Indecent exposure. Fear, shame, hiding, paranoia.

While I wanted out, I didn't know how. I had tried so many times, only to be squeezed more tightly, like a python squeezes her squirming victim until they surrender the fight. It felt like I was suffocating in silence. My voice didn't seem to matter to him or to anyone around me. While I'd been pressed and demanded to become a sexual object, I hid. I had been objectified and fetishized, and it made me sick every waking moment of my life. No one noticed my pain. My cries for help went unnoticed and unattended-to. I was bound by insecurity, silenced my shame, and bound by depression. He was toxic, that's for sure. But he was all I had.

He led me beside a short tree. We sat on the prickly brown grass, pretending that it wasn't so bad. The summer heat still beat down, causing him to smell of fabric softener and musky sweat. I stalled with talk, but he commenced with touch. We were stationed on the edge of the field, aside a crickety fence behind someone's house. *Would someone catch us?* I wondered. I hoped to be **rescued**, *not* humiliated. I swallowed, my tongue capped with the taste of anxiety. He groped and touched me as I looked around nervously. He spoke profanities over me and my body, belittling my existence. He was sexually aggressive and unapologetic about it. My stomach turned as he continued to further compromise my clothes.

"I don't want anyone to see us," I pleaded.

"It will be fine," he responded, careless to the risk and negligent to my fears.

He continued to compromise. Without much active participation of my own, my body had been fondled and handled. I stopped engaging. Eventually, I found myself face-down on the prickly grass, partly exposed. The only thing that shielded me was his body hovering over. I felt helpless. After his traveled conquest of my body, he was finally ready to take his pursuits to the next level. I tried to cover myself again, and he exposed me more. I felt him behind me, ready to go. I couldn't do it. I just *couldn't*.

"Stop," I said, softly.

He pressed my body into the ground. (*Maybe he didn't hear me.*)

"Stop!" I said, louder.

He penetrated. (*Did he ignore me?*)

"NO!" I said in a yelp. (*Oh. He's doing this on purpose.*)

I squirmed to move from under him, but he let his body weight anchor me down. He began pumping into me shamelessly, without regard to my voice. It hurt, badly. It was almost too painful to bear, yet I had no choice but to endure it. I looked around from ground view, wondering if this was truly happening to me.

I froze.

I was in so much pain, embarrassed and overtaken.

And it kept going.

And going.

This episode was taking longer than I thought.

I felt the physical pain, but didn't have the will to fight. I zoned out of my body and went numb. When my body turned off, by mind flicked on. I became strangely lucid. I was able to look around and think clearly. It was as if time fizzled down to slow-motion. I saw a man walking by the field. He didn't look our way. It's funny that I was undergoing one of the most traumatic moments of my life, and the man was walking by obliviously.

Why didn't I have the courage to leave when my stomach was turning half an hour ago? I knew something bad was going to happen today. Why had I let it get this far? Why was it so hard to leave? I figured that I deserved to be here. *I asked for this.*

He finished.

I put my clothes on quietly. I held back tears. I knew that he could see my countenance, but I knew he didn't care. He was casual and peppy, as to not spook me. He didn't acknowledge it, and neither did I. We walked back to school, hand-in-hand like nothing ever happened. *Was I really just raped?* I asked myself. I knew I had been, but I couldn't make sense of it at all. *Did he know what he just did?* I wasn't sure.

When we arrived back, he laughed and joked casually with his friends while I hovered around like a ghost. I didn't talk about it with him. I didn't talk about it with friends. I didn't talk about it with parents. I didn't tell anyone. For years.

Until this morning, at 4am with my two friends.

For the first time, I used my words to share with them the horrific event that took place over 7 years prior. When I told them, my words were pieced and jumbled. It was hardly coherent, but they seemed to understand it all. I felt like a liar, pretending to be the victim.

"God wants you to know that it's not your fault." One friend said.

Wow. I never imagined hearing those words.

For over seven years, I had convinced myself that it was *my fault*. I had reasoned that if it weren't, then what would possess me to stay with him? It was hard to admit to myself that I was so bound. I had become conditioned to accept shame and blame. I rationalized the dysfunction instead of recognizing my value. It had become so unhealthy and toxic that I felt powerless to move on. It felt so freeing that someone else would affirm that the pain I experienced *was not my fault*.

The Healing Begins

This took a turning point in my healing journey. Confessing to myself that I had been sexually assaulted was the first step. Then, confessing it to my friends at 4am was the next step. I then confessed this deep-seated pain to my husband. Then, I shared my testimony with women that I mentored. Lastly, I shared it with my dad. Now, I can confidently say that I am free from the effects of feeling voiceless, objectified, and compromised by another person.

While that may sound like a peachy and speedy happy ending, it took me 9 years—from the time I was in that High School relationship until the time where I was able to sense freedom—to get to that place of restoration. That healing process from that toxic relationship was particularly long for me because for most of those years, I was silent. I told everyone that I had "been in a toxic relationship," but I wasn't upfront about the extent of that toxicity. That mentality may have spared them, but it sabotaged me. In order to heal, I needed to open my mouth.

James 5:16 says, "Confess your sins to each other and pray for each other so that you may be healed." Now, the phrase *your sins* has a connotation of personal offense; sins that *you* have inflicted on yourself or on others. But think about it this way: what if you were also responsible to confess the sins inflicted upon you? After all, those feel like "your sins," too. Trauma and pain become a part of you if they go unaddressed and unconfessed. For instance, if you've been sexually mishandled, you might begin to take on the identity of "dirty" or "used." You internalize that sin against you and may even become sexually provocative yourself. Sin done against you is just as toxic, so confess *all* sin. Every sin. The sins others have inflicted upon you, the sins you have inflicted upon others, and the sins that you've inflicted upon yourself. *Confess*.

Confession cannot be done in the absence of community. Notice that that scripture in James didn't say, "confess your sins to God." While it's imperative that you confess your sins to God and repent, know that you'll find true healing in *community*. The scripture says "confess your sins to *each other* and pray for *each other* so that you may be *healed*." In other words, don't expect to experience healing without confession in community. You can determine whether or not you extend your healing process. If you want to experience true freedom from the deepest pains in your life, then you'll need to share them.

Types of Wounds
Different types of wounds require different time periods for healing. This is true both physically and emotionally. Let's use physical wounds as an example. Depending on the healing time of a physical wound, it can be classified as *acute* or *chronic*. **Acute wounds** normally come about suddenly

and unexpectedly, and heal without complication in the expected amount of time. *Think scrapes, cuts, and punctures.* These can range from superficial scratches to deep wounds.

A **chronic wound** develops when an acute doesn't heal in the predicted amount of time. This delay in healing can be caused by a lack of the main requirements of healing, such as a healthy supply of blood, a healthy supply of oxygen and nutrients, and a clean and infection-free environment. In order to treat wounds, you need to remove the thing that is slowing down the healing, namely *constant pressure.* When wounds do not get relief from constant pressure, there can be a breakdown of the tissue. *

This sounds a lot like a poorly-treated emotional wound, too. Many of us have dealt with unattended emotional wounds that stick around long past their inception. Do you have the pressure of silence or the pressure to "just get over it," causing a wound to linger? Does it feel as if you've had pain building up over time, unrelenting until you eventually break down? Do you have any emotional wounds that are *chronic*?

You may be thinking, *how do I know that I have an emotionally chronic wound?*

Well, think about it this way: an acute wound will hurt for a season, but then you'll move on, grow, and get better. However, if the pain of your past has been plaguing you for years, has no end in sight, and you haven't grown from it, then it is a chronic wound. Whether it was the trauma of your childhood, the sting of unexpected church hurt, or the penetrating words of a friend, if it's lingering long past its due date, then the wound needs to be treated *immediately*.

An emotional wound that's **acute** requires healthy confession among healthy community. It requires intentional care and regular precaution. It may require you a few venting sessions, crying spells, and mental health days. You could even seek Christian counseling and therapy. You will certainly need a heavy emphasis on scripture, prayer, fasting, worship, and journaling. With proper care, you can treat this. You'll get over this. You'll find freedom.

An emotional wound that's **chronic** requires you to treat it in the same way that you'd treat an acute one, except you have to take one more step: **you have to address the agent that is causing the healing delay**. The thing triggering the delay could be your lack of healthy confession, lack of forgiveness for yourself and/or others, or even you subjecting yourself to an environment that easily triggers you, hindering your capacity to grow. Whatever the thing is, tackle that first. If you need to confess, confess. If you need to forgive, forgive. If you need to protect yourself, then protect yourself. Do whatever it takes to seek full healing and freedom from your past. The truth is that you'll never emerge as the woman that God has called you to be without first shedding your cover of pain.

PAIN ISN'T WHO YOU ARE

Pain has a way of becoming our identifier. It's easy to do. Think about how often we label people by their pain before their name. We'll say,

"the mentally-ill person"

"the handicapped girl"

"that heavy-set guy"

"the homeless person"

"the leper,"

In fact there's a particular woman of great faith in the Bible who was notoriously labeled by her pain. We know her as, "the woman with the issue of blood." My favorite account of this passage in the Bible is in Luke 8:43-48. Here's the story:

> *A woman in the crowd had suffered for twelve years with constant bleeding, and she could find no cure. Coming up behind Jesus, she touched the fringe of his robe. Immediately, the bleeding stopped.*
> *"Who touched me?" Jesus asked.*
>
> *Everyone denied it, and Peter said, "Master, this whole crowd is pressing up against you."*

But Jesus said, "Someone deliberately touched me, for I felt healing power go out from me." When the woman realized that she could not stay hidden, she began to tremble and fell to her knees in front of him. The whole crowd heard her explain why she had touched him and that she had been immediately healed. "Daughter," he said to her, "your faith has made you well. Go in peace."

This brave woman had been plagued with chronic bleeding for twelve years, and others knew it. People identified her by her pain. Despite the duration of her ailment, she believed she could be well if she could simply encounter Jesus. Rather than being bound by the familiarity of her label, she desperately reached for the One who could redefine her. The moment she touched the fringe of Jesus' robe, her pain ceased. In an instant, she was healed. There is a principle at play here: if you reach for healing—no matter how long you've been defined by your pain—Jesus is able to heal you in a moment.

There is another principle at play in this scripture. At the end of this passage, when Jesus finally lays eyes on the woman He healed, He calls her "Daughter." This woman had been labeled by others as, "the woman with the issue of blood," but God didn't see her that way. Jesus immediately identified her as "Daughter." The first miracle Jesus performed was healing her; the greater miracle He performed was identifying her. She was no longer her pain; she was a daughter of God. It was her identity that allowed her to "go in peace." The woman may have been healed physically, but if her whole body was destined to eternal separation from God, then what good would that be? Jesus not only healed her from her physical issue, but He also resolved her spiritual issue. She no longer belonged to her pain of this world—she belonged to God.

If you've had a pain that has been plaguing your life for longer than you'd like to admit, then you're in good company. If wear the badge of "depressed," "victim," "abused," "forgotten," "rejected," "insufficient," "ugly," "wounded," "anxious," "crazy," "sick," or anything other than the name "Daughter," then it's time for you to reach for Jesus. It's time for you to shed the labels that pain has given you so that you can be identified only by your relation to the Almighty God. The God who made the universe, galaxies, solar systems, planets, nations, cities, people, insects, sand, atoms, and subatomic particles not only knows you, but He identifies you as HIS. You are not depressed, victimized, abused, forgotten, rejected, insufficient, ugly wounded, anxious, crazy, sick, or anything else in the eyes of God. You are *Daughter*.

So shed the labels. I know that it may be difficult to believe that you could be anything other than your labels, but you can. I know that it may be hard to believe that you could be healed in an instant after years of pain, but you can. If you will face your fears and confront the pain that's plagued you for so long, you can decide to be courageous enough to trust Jesus to alleviate the burden.

Recall all of the names that have identified you other than "Daughter." Call out the names that others have given you, the names enemy has suggested to you, or even the names that you've self-identified as. Be honest with yourself about this. Then, pray to Jesus. The scripture says that, "by His stripes we are healed." Ask God, "What would it practically take for me to *reach* for your healing?" Write down whatever the Holy Spirit reveals to you. It may require forgiveness. It may require counseling. It may require a tough conversation with a parent. It may even simply require your prayer of faith. Resolve that you will be obedient to whatever God shows you. Then, ask God to heal you as you're diligent to reach for Him.

Lastly, accept that your name is Daughter. Your name is not sickness, pain, or failure. It is not fearful, unfaithful, or sinful. It is Daughter. Declare that you are His Daughter and choose to walk in peace.

SHED ACTION PLAN

The second stage of a butterfly's life cycle is the caterpillar stage. During this stage, the caterpillar spends its time eating, sleeping, and growing. When a caterpillar becomes too large for its skin, it molts, or sheds its skin. It goes through this shedding process 4-6 times before it enters into its next phase of life.

If a caterpillar weren't shedding its outer layers, that would be a sign that the caterpillar wasn't growing. That's much like us, isn't it? If we were wearing the same identifiers that we wore when we were teenagers, it would be a sign that we're not growing. If you were bullied when you were five years old, then you owe it to yourself to shed the pain of that as you mature in age.

The second stage of The Life Cycle of Change is SHED. In this stage, you consume all that is pushing you toward your destiny and you shed all that is hindering you from it. This is the stage that so many Christians stay stuck in—trapped in unforgiveness, shame, limiting beliefs, and more. Remaining trapped in your caterpillar skin doesn't disqualify you from salvation, but it certainly does hinder you from fulfilling your calling.

Galatians 5:1 says,

> *It is for freedom that Christ has set us free. Stand firm, then, and do not let yourselves be burdened again by a yoke of slavery.*

God sent Jesus to die for our freedom. He doesn't want us bound to our past, our inner critic, our fear, or our wounds. If He were content with us living in depression, lust, and bitterness, then God would have never sent Jesus to rescue us from the obligation to it. The scripture is clear that we have been set free from sin; however, we shed the mindset of slavery and sin little by little, season by season. As we grow in the knowledge of scripture, in our relationship with Christ, and in healthy community, we become so large in the Spirit that our old ways of thinking, believing, feeling, and acting go away. Understand that the *Shed* stage of the Life Cycle of Change is not passive—it's active. It's aggressive. It won't happen by osmosis. This is why you'll see 50-year old people who are still bitter, immature, and angry—they hold onto beliefs and hurts from when they were 12 years old. Shedding is serious business. It requires intentionality about what you pick up and bravery with what you lay down. You have the power to decide that you will grow, shed, develop, and change.

EMOTIONAL HEALING

If you've struggled to confess your hurts to others, then start with confessing to yourself. It's hard to confront what you won't admit to yourself. Instead of sparing your feelings and delaying your healing process, be brutally honest with yourself for once: what is the core emotion associated with your wound?

Whatever the pain that follows you is, there is a core emotion associated with it. What hurt lies beneath your fears and frustrations? It may be rejection, abandonment, betrayal, sadness, failure, worthlessness, emptiness, shame, resentment, anger, loneliness, or anything else. Whatever it is, admit that to yourself. If you're having trouble identifying the pain, ask the Holy Spirit to reveal it to you.

Perhaps you've been feeling plagued by feelings of rejection. Every time you enter into a new friendship, you fear that the friends will reject who you are. You build up a facade of who you think they'll like. Without fail, it seems as if you're never enough. Friendships fizzle out. People leave you. And you're left feeling inadequate, wounded, and rejected.

Once you've identified the pain, then walk through the steps of emotional healing. Let's use **rejection** as an example:

1. **Admit that you feel rejected.** At the top of a piece of paper, write down the word "rejection." Tell yourself that you feel rejected, and then tell God that you feel rejected. Rather than ignoring the pain, be present to it.

2. **Think back to the very first time you ever felt rejected.** (It could be as late as last year, or as early as three years old. All that matters is that you indicate the very first time you felt rejected. Replay and relive that moment. Remember details you may have forgotten.)

   Write down the painful accounts of rejection you recall, from earliest to most recent. Once you have a rolodex of rejection stories, you can see where your pain was introduced and reinforced. You may pick up on a pattern, and it may be tough to acknowledge. But here is your chance; you can finally be honest with yourself.

3. **Ask for God to reveal to you the truth about these situations**. Here is your opportunity to open yourself up to the voice of the Holy Spirit. Ask God a question, and give Him room to answer. Sit in silence, and take note of everything that you see, hear, notice, imagine, remember, sense, and feel. This is God communicating with you. He wants to reveal to you more about His love for you and His plan for you. Write down whatever He reveals to you, and don't question it.

4. **Forgive the offender**. Who caused you feelings of rejection? Write their name(s) down. Do you self-reject? Write your own name down. Then, release these people, one at a time. Forgiveness isn't a feeling, it's an action. It's resolving not to hold a grudge, harbor resentment, cling to hatred, or withhold love. Say out loud, "I forgive — — —," and then pray for their well-being and healing (even if this person is you).

5. **Ask Jesus to replace the pain with something better**. If you could replace the feeling of rejection

with any other positive emotion, what would it be? Perhaps you'd rather replace feelings of rejection with feelings of **acceptance**. Maybe what you truly desire is a strong sense of **worthiness**. Don't simply reach for any emotion; desire the emotion that would truly satisfy the void in your heart. Then, ask Jesus, "Jesus, your scripture says that by your stripes I am healed. So please heal me. Replace my feelings of rejection with feelings of — — —."

Lastly, assess how you feel. Are the negative feelings gone? Do you feel lighter? Oftentimes, this process for emotional healing brings about feelings of ease, as if a burden has been lifted. If this isn't the case, then that is an indication that there is another negative emotion at play in addition to the emotion of rejection. Once the primary emotion is dealt with, it often reveals another underlying emotion that has been simmering all the while. It may be unworthiness, abandonment, or anything else. Identify that emotion immediately and then go through the process of emotional healing again. Continue to do this until you feel a change.

STAGE THREE

DEVELOP

HIDDEN HOUSEWIFE

I scrubbed the dishes, face bowed in attempts that Jasmine wouldn't see my face. I was choked up, bent out of shape, holding back tears. I felt empty as a stay-at-home-mom. I had left my job as a music teacher in Dallas, TX, a career in which I excelled in, to pursue a life as Suzy homemaker in the new city of Atlanta, GA. I had nothing to call my own—no money, no career, no titles... *nothing*. I wasn't known as Amanda. I was known as Michael's wife and Bean's mom. People around me usually addressed *them* before they acknowledged me. I thought that this life was what I wanted, but I didn't realize how humbling it would be. My days consisted of washing dishes, changing diapers, nursing my son, and doing laundry. I was trapped in the mundane, wondering if I would ever make an impact outside of my home. I believed that I had much to offer the world, but I was hidden.

Even though I didn't want to talk, we did. Jasmine saw straight through me. She lived with us at the time, so she saw my not-so-Instagram-worthy moments. I shared with her some of the pains that I was going through. I felt so vulnerable sharing my heart with her. I didn't want to come off as ungrateful for everything that I had already been given—a husband, a child, a house, and the opportunity to live a simple life. But she didn't judge me. She welcomed me and listened. She suspected that I was struggling with my identity. She mentioned that a friend of hers had recently prompted her to ask God the way that He saw her. She said that God gave her a special name—His *Warrior Princess*.

I thought that I was pretty spiritual. I thought that I was pretty mature. Yet why had I never sat down to ask God the way that He saw me? The concept seemed so simple. Why hadn't this thought ever crossed my mind? I resolved that I needed to know His name for me. Soon after, I went to my room. I grabbed a journal and a pen and cozied myself on my bed. I bowed my head in reverence as I entered into the presence of God.

"God, I just want to hear you. You know how I've been feeling. I'm lonely. I'm feeling insecure. I feel lost. I give all of that to you right now. I clear my head. All I want is to hear your voice. All I want is to know the way that YOU see me. I don't want to care about the way that the world sees me... I just need to hear from you. So I'll ask, and then I'm going to listen."

"...God, *how do you see me?*"

The room fell silent. I felt still. I heard my breaths. Then, thoughts of wonder swarmed through my mind. *Would God speak?* I questioned.

Again, I shook my head. I cleared my mind. I wouldn't doubt. I needed to hear this from my Father.

Then, thoughts came to my mind. Thoughts that I didn't actively think. Thoughts that I didn't have to conjure up. Thoughts that didn't sound like me. Thoughts that came from God.

"You're my Treasure," I heard God say.

I was stunned.

"I have entrusted you because I trust in you." He continued.

A picture of a treasure chest with valuable, glimmering gems entrusted to it filled my mind. He saw me as a trust, like a safe for His word, His truth, His wisdom, and His purpose. I wrote every word down onto the paper, not wanting to add or take away from anything He said. I was overwhelmed with joy and gratitude. God *really* saw me this way? I held that much value to God? He calls me His treasure? I'm often told to trust God, but *God* trusts *me*?

"God, what am I called to do?" I asked, not wanting to miss a word.

"You're anointed to preach, to pray and to prophesy."

Again, I was shocked by the words.

While I had spoken at a few gigs prior and I had filmed a few YouTube videos, I was never confident that I was called to speak, let alone *preach*. I just thought that speaking was a space that I may have wanted to dabble in, but I was never sure if it was *my* desire or God's desire. I often shied away from the notion of preaching and speaking because I never wanted to be someone who was looking for a mic. I never wanted to seek a platform or admiration. I knew that if I were to ever pursue preaching, it would have to be because God led me to do it. I was certain that my husband was called to preach—he had been speaking since he was young, and he had just began preaching at our church. Everyone admired and affirmed His position and gift. He went on to be ordained as a teacher and later became a pastor. But I never knew that I was anointed to preach. I hadn't considered myself a candidate. This was the first time that my voice as a preacher had ever been affirmed and validated—before I even began preaching.

And, I was anointed to pray! I didn't know that there could even be an anointing to pray. I honestly didn't know what that meant or what to do with that. All I knew was that I needed to begin praying even more. And *prophesying...* Wow! I was familiar with tapping into the voice of God, and every time that I was obedient to that voice, it turned out in my favor. However, I hadn't used the gift for the benefit of other people. I was too timid to risk being wrong. I had been enamored with others' prophetic gifts, neglecting to honor my own anointing to prophesy. I was startled by the words, but I didn't question them. I simply believed that I was who God said I was. I knew that I had work to do!

After this day, my season didn't change, but my attitude did. I was still hidden. I was still Michael's wife and Bean's mom. I was still cleaning the house and changing diapers. But I knew who I was and I knew what I was called to do. Because I knew who I was, I started stewarding my identity in private. Nobody saw me, but I would stroll my son around our neighborhood as I interceded on behalf of the entire block. I prayed for families to be mended, chains to be broken, and I prophesied life back into the schools. I also joined the prayer team at my church, waking up early each day to pray for our church, our pastors, and our nation.

I began prophesying to women around me, even risking being wrong. I knew that I had to start somewhere. I didn't say, "thus saith the Lord." I simply told them that I'm looking to steward and sharpen my prophetic gift. That gift began to grow and develop, until I became very competent in hearing God's voice. One day, I wrote a prophetic letter to each woman in my 20-piece small group. Many of the women I didn't personally know. A few of them I had never had a conversation with before. However, God led me to prophesy, so I did. That night, the whole room of women were brought to tears by the words that God spoke to them through me. After that day, I resolved that I would keep prophesying. It became about the lives that I could touch, and it was no longer about my own perfection.

I eventually went on the preach more frequently online, at speaking engagements and at my church. And when

I did, I never had to question my position. I knew that I wasn't misaligned with God's will for my life, because He told me that I was anointed to preach. When you know what you're made to do, you hold your head up higher. You deliver your message with confidence. You don't second-guess or self-doubt. You know who you are and what you're called to do, so you do it.

DEVELOP IN HIDING

You were placed on earth on purpose for a purpose. You weren't born to simply take in all that life has to offer. No, your hope should be to leave the world better off than what you left it. Ephesians 2:10 says that "we are God's handiwork, created in Christ Jesus to do good works, which God prepared in advance for us to do." This means that God has placed a ministry in you that no one else can take or accomplish. Before you were even born, God had a destiny and a calling in mind for you. Being hidden won't forfeit your ministry to someone who is in the spotlight. Being hidden won't change your design. Being hidden won't hinder your destiny. You have a role and a function to fulfil in every season of your life—even in the seasons in which you're hidden.

Being hidden is often a season that welcomes growth, processing, and development. God will entrust you with more, but He wants to ensure that your gifts, talents, skill sets, and character have the capacity to sustain it. God will often hide you for a season to affirm your identity, show you your destiny, and develop your character. If you're surrounded by darkness and obscurity, wondering when it will be "your time" to be elevated to a place of leadership, higher-level influence, and visibility, you're likely in Stage Three of The Life Cycle of Change—*Develop*. Understand that the Develop stage is not your destination; it is simply a part of the journey.

We all go through this stage at various levels until we see change in our lives. You don't only undergo the Develop stage once in your life and then shine in the spotlight for the rest of eternity. What will happen is that you'll go through a similar season every time you're going to reach a higher level of exposure and influence. This happens because God is more concerned with your character than He is with your capacity. He wants to ensure that if He is going to give you more to steward, you not only are capable, but you also have outstanding character.

Throughout the Bible, God hides His most influential servants: Joseph was hidden in a pit, and again in a prison before he was ultimately promoted to the palace. Moses was hidden in the desert for a third of his life before he led the Israelites into the Promised Land. David was hidden in the mountains and the fields before he was chosen and crowned as king. Elijah was hidden at Cherith before his great life contribution at Carmel. Paul was hidden for three years in Arabia after his conversion, before he became a missionary. Even Jesus was hidden to develop for 30 years of His life, and then was hidden again in the wilderness for 40 days to be tested before He entered into His public ministry and was revealed to the world as Messiah. If you're called to accomplish great things, then expect for God to hide you first. If God did it to Jesus, then He will do it to you. When God hides you for a season, He's developing you for significance.

DEVELOP YOUR CHARACTER

The development that is done in private will ultimately make its appearance in public. This reminds me of when I used to play flute. Flute was once a huge part of my life. I played the flute from the time I was in 6th grade, all the way throughout college, where I received my degree in Music Education. I was often first or second chair, and I went on to be second place in the Texas All-State band for 4A division, and one of the top chairs in the 5A division. I was used to auditioning and getting solos and having my chance to *shine*. But do you know what took place well before all of that? Hours of obscurity. Hours of isolation. Hours in the practice room. I would practice and practice and practice by myself, until my fingers would have marks on them from holding my flute. I would develop my sound practicing long tones. I would develop my rhythmic accuracy subdividing with a metronome. I would develop my ear by recording myself and playing it back. I would develop my technique by playing complicated etudes and scales with all sorts of variants and accidentals. I'd spend days self-assessing, practicing the same four measures over and over again until every finger glitch, tone disruption and improper dynamic was corrected.

No one cheered me on whenever I was so frustrated that I wanted to throw my flute against the wall. But my consistency with practicing and developing in private prepared me for the moment when it all counted: audition time. Every time that I would face an audition—the place of testing—I was confident. I didn't feel as if I was "performing" whenever I was auditioning. Why should I have? I had played the same excerpt 400 times before. I practiced the way I would perform. Testing reveals your level of preparation. And I was prepared.

While the musical development that was done in private was frustrating, it all paid off in the end. Some payoffs included my placement in the All State band, Principal flutist of the Youth Orchestra of Greater Fort Worth, first place in a highly-esteemed solo competition, and my ultimate admittance into the highly-esteemed university of my dreams, SMU in Dallas. While I no longer pursue music, the principle remains the same. The developmental work that you consistently commit to in private will ultimately show itself in public.

The difference between your season of hiding and my time of development while playing the flute is that I was developing *capability*, but you will be developing *character*. In the same way that we work to refine a skill, God wants to work to refine our character. We develop in the frustration and obscurity of hiding. No one feels our silent struggles. No one sees us hurt and grow. We prepare for the destiny and call that God has shown us, and we do it without praise or applause. We do it to the glory of God. Then, when a time of testing comes, what is within us is revealed. All of the soul work that we have done exposes us, and we pass the test. After we endure testing for some time, we're trusted with more.

Paul describes the tense and tiresome process of developing character in 1 Corinthians 9:24-27:

> *Do you not know that in a race all the runners run, but only one gets the prize? Run in such a way as to get the prize. Everyone who competes in the games goes into strict training. They do it to get a crown that will not last, but we do it to get a crown that will last forever. Therefore I do not run like someone running aimlessly; I do not fight like a boxer beating the air. No, I strike a blow to my body and make it my slave so that after I have preached to others, I myself will not be disqualified for the prize.*

Private development can feel like what Paul mentions—striking blows to your body to make it your slave.

Spiritually, mentally, emotionally, physically... development hurts. It costs you your comfort. It costs you your selfish desires. It costs you your pride. You have to train your flesh to submit under the authority of the Holy Spirit. You have to say "no" to the wrong thing, and "yes" to the right thing. In the end, it's worth it. As Paul mentions, we do it to get a crown that will last forever. Beauty fades. Status fades. Prestige fades. Money fades. But after everything is stripped away, what cannot be taken away from you is your character. You bring that with you into eternity.

Scripture tells us that we will all give an account to God. At the end of your life, you will stand before God. There, God will evaluate how well you loved, served, and developed. God won't assess *what* you did; He will evaluate *why* you did. God looks at the heart—our intentions behind our actions. Paul says in 1 Corinthians 4 says,

> *Now, a person who is put in charge as a manager must be faithful. As for me, it matters very little how I might be evaluated by you or by any human authority. I*

don't even trust my own judgment on this point. My conscience is clear, but that doesn't prove I'm right. It is the Lord himself who will examine me and decide. So don't make judgments about anyone ahead of time—before the Lord returns. For he will bring our darkest secrets to light and will reveal our private motives. Then God will give to each one whatever praise is due.

When our motives are tested on Judgement Day, it is like our grand audition day. Our preparation in private is revealed for heaven to see. If we were diligent to develop in the fruit of the Spirit—love, joy, peace, patience, kindness, goodness, faithfulness, gentleness, and self-control—and our motives were pure, we will be rewarded. If our motives were impure and we failed to develop, we won't be. Just let that sink in.

While we have the ability to be capable without having character, if you do so, you'll regret it. Whether you are exposed to the masses, experience moral failure, or even worse—you stand before God in painful remorse, failure to develop simply isn't worth it. There are highly skilled and gifted people on platforms that they don't belong on, hurting people in the process. Having public position without a developed character only places those people in a high place of vulnerability, only to be brought low when it is revealed that they are not who they claim to be. Don't be so eager to earn a place of honor before you truly deserve it. One scripture that explains this well is in Luke 14:8-11:

> When someone invites you to a wedding feast, do not take the place of honor, for a person more distinguished than you may have been invited. If so, the host who invited both of you will come and say to you, 'Give this person your seat.' Then, humiliated, you will have to take the least important place. But when you are invited, take the lowest place, so that when your host comes, he will say to you, 'Friend, move up to a better place.' Then you will be honored in the presence of all the other guests. For all those who exalt themselves will be humbled, and those who humble themselves will be exalted.

It's better to be promoted than to be demoted. Who wants the humiliation of being demoted because you seated yourself in a place of honor before you truly deserved to be there? God does not owe you anything, so don't feel entitled to a position that you didn't earn. Think of this concept whenever you're in the *Develop* stage. Your season of development requires *humility*. It is a time of being hidden and a time of being humbled. Don't rush this season to quickly achieve a place of honor; develop as much as you can in this season so that you can become the person you need to be in order to sustain the place of honor when the time of promotion comes. When you're hidden and humble, you'll know that when you're honored, it will be because of your heart, and not just your hustle. You'll rest assured knowing that you didn't manipulate the mantle. Because you grew to that place and you didn't swell to that place, your growth and your seat of honor will be maintained. You won't be demoted, because while you were in hiding, you were diligent to develop.

DEVELOP ACTION PLAN

Butterflies are nature's showpiece, exhibiting their art with every flap of their delicate wings. When we see butterflies, we see an emblem of beauty. Designed for display, we admire the butterfly in its fully-grown glory. It's easy to adore the allure of a butterfly without applauding the development that it took to become. In the same way that a caterpillar is destined to be a butterfly, a butterfly will always have the essence of a caterpillar. They're distinctly different, yet one in the same. The two bodies collide and transact in the third stage of their life. This transformative stage is not public; it takes place in the dark. The caterpillar undergoes this dark phase of its life cycle inside of what is called a **chrysalis**. This is commonly referred to as a pupa.

From the shell of the pupa, it appears as if the caterpillar is resting, but inside of the pupa is where all of the action is. First, the caterpillar releases enzymes to dissolve all of its tissues and digests itself. Organized cell groups known as imaginal discs survive the digestive process. A caterpillar has an imaginal disc for every adult body part it will need as a mature butterfly —discs for its eyes, for its wings, its legs and more. Once a caterpillar has digested all of its tissues except for the imaginal discs, those discs undergo rapid cell division that form the wings, antennae, legs, eyes, and all the other features of an adult butterfly. *

This is much like the third stage Life Cycle of Change—*Develop*. This stage is all about how you relate to yourself while faced with yourself. Rather than undergoing a public change, you look inwardly and privately to rapidly digest all that you used to be, morphing you into the woman you were always destined to be. The Holy Spirit works like imaginal discs within you, being the essential catalyst that births newness.

While in the hidden place of development, you take time to learn about the way that you were created—your spiritual gifts, your passions, your abilities, your personality, and your experiences. You become a student of yourself, and that sparks immense growth. During this stage, you are tested, refined, and prepared. You develop in your character, capability, and capacity. As believers, we are constantly developing. You'll find that the *Develop* stage isn't a one-

and-done stage of the cycle, but a stage that we go through to break through to each higher level of authority in our lives and calling. Follow the *Develop Action Plan* so that you can steward this stage with direction, clarity and insight.

WHAT DOES GOD CALL YOU?

It's not enough for me to tell you the amazing story about how God named me His "Treasure." God has a special name that He calls *you*. Throughout scripture, names have significance. In fact, there are many instances in which God gives new names to His people. He renamed Abram to Abraham, Jacob to Israel, Sarai to Sarah, Saul to Paul, Simon to Peter, and more. He does this because He wants to identify us by His standards and not the world's. Even in the book of Revelation 2:17, it reads,

> *To him who overcomes I will give some of the hidden manna to eat. And I will give him a white stone, and on the stone a new name written, which no one knows except him who receives it.*

This passage is telling us that every believer will be given a new name when we're glorified in heaven. While there is much to be taken into account for this scripture in order to understand it's contextual complexities, the principle that we can take away from it is this: God cares about your name. He cares about it so much that He's planning to give you a new one at the end of the age.

If you're in a season of development and you need a stronger sense of identity, then I challenge you to ask God how He sees you. Ask Him if He has a special name for you. If God has a special name that He wants to reveal to you now, then if you ask Him, He will tell you. If God does not want to reveal to you a special name that He has for you now, then He won't. It's that simple!

After you ask God to reveal to you how He views you, including any name that He gives you, write it down and date it. This is your *true* identity. While you're tucked away in the obscurity of development, remember your name. Amidst the struggle of measuring up to the expectations of others, remember how God sees you. When you're lacking direction and clarity, remember that what you do flows out of who you are; and *this* is who you are.

As Daughters of God, here are some ways that we are identified in scripture:

Child of God (John 1:12)

Branch of the True Vine (John 15:1, 5)

Friend of Jesus (John 15:15)

Justified and redeemed (Romans 3:24)

Set free from sin and death (Romans 8:2)

Co-heir with Christ (Romans 8:17)

Accepted by Christ (Romans 15:7)

Called to be a saint (1 Corinthians 1:2). (See also Ephesians 1:1, Philippians 1:1, and Colossians 1:2.)

A temple of the Holy Spirit (1 Corinthians 6:19)

One spirit with God (1 Corinthians 6:17)

A new creation (2 Corinthians 5:17)

The righteousness of God (2 Corinthians 5:21)

No longer a slave, but a child and an heir (Galatians 4:7)

Set free in Christ (Galatians 5:1)

Chosen, holy, and blameless before God (Ephesians 1:4)

Redeemed and forgiven by the grace of Christ (Ephesians 1:7)

God's own possession (Ephesians 1:11)

Sealed with the Holy Spirit (Ephesians 1:13)

Alive with Christ (Ephesians 2:4-5)

Seated in the heavenly places with Christ (Ephesians 2:6)

God's workmanship (Ephesians 2:10)

Member of Christ's body (Ephesians 3:6)(Ephesians 5:30)

A citizen of heaven (Philippians 3:20)

Complete in Christ (Colossians 2:10)

Chosen of God, holy and beloved (Colossians 3:12)

Loved and chosen by God (1 Thessalonians 1:4)

BAPTISM OF THE HOLY SPIRIT

"You'd never guess what I did today," Michael said while sitting beside me in the driver's seat.

"What?" I asked.

"Today when I was with Ben, I got baptized by the Holy Spirit."

"Oh, did he dunk you in water?" I inquired, thinking it a little spontaneous and strange.

"Not baptized in water... I got baptized by the Holy Spirit. I started speaking in tongues." He responded eagerly.

"YOU SPOKE IN TONGUES?!" I responded, flabbergasted.

"Yeah, it was crazy!"

"I've never heard of the baptism of the Holy Spirit. I don't think that's in the Bible." I said, cautiously. I thought that there was only one baptism. This is the one recognized by being fully submerged under water by a pastoral figure, to be raised up dripping in victory. I had to have been super-saved, because I was water baptized twice—once when I was seven, and later when I was nineteen. So when my husband

and then boyfriend, Michael, told me about being baptized with the Holy Spirit, I thought he was deranged.

"It is. Ben walked me through the purple book. It's all there. I can show you."

Michael proceeded to tell me about how there were multiple scriptures that talk about the baptism of the Holy Spirit, and how we're supposed to get baptized both by water AND by the Holy Spirit. I was unsure about everything, but incredibly intrigued.

"Do you want to be baptized too?" Michael finally asked.

I was nervous. Would I speak in tongues? I had never heard *tongues* before. Would anything happen? Would the Holy Spirit possess me? What is this all for? What's the meaning behind this all?

"Yes, let's do it!" I responded. I had so many questions, but I wanted what he had.

After that, Michael and I went back to his college dorm room. He walked me through all of the same scriptures that Ben—Michael's discipler—walked Michael through before his baptism. I was blown away by how detailed and plain this concept was. After going through the scriptures, I understood clearly that I was supposed to be baptized again—this time not by water but by *fire*.

I was ready to experience God in a new and fresh way. I wanted to feel Him. I wanted to know His presence. I wanted to have a supernatural encounter that no one else could refute or take away. And that is exactly what happened.

Michael placed his hand on my head, and began to pray for me. He told me to ask God to baptize me in the Holy Spirit.

"God, your Word says that you are a good Father and you give good gifts—including your Spirit. So I pray that you don't withhold this from me. Please baptize me by fire and allow me to experience your power."

Michael began speaking in tongues. I held my hands open-faced, demonstratively positioned to receive all of the spiritual blessing that God was preparing to release to me. I began to feel warmth surrounding me. Then, the hottest energy radiated, not from around me but from within me. In a matter of minutes, heat radiated from my lower back and traveled up my arms through my fingertips. My hands felt buzzy. There was an electric, tingly sensation that insinuated that energy was pulsing out from my fingertips. I felt like I was super-charged with spiritual energy that was so powerful that it physically manifested.

All of this happened while I was praying to God.

I told Michael what was happening. He asked me if I desired to speak in tongues. "Yes, but I'm nervous," I responded.

Michael said, "The Holy Spirit gives utterance."

"The Holy Spirit gives utterance," I said confidently. I knew God could do anything at this moment, because I was overcome by the overwhelming glory of His presence.

"You may feel as if you'll want to say something. If so, don't hold back."

I was self-conscious. I didn't want to fake anything, but what I was experiencing was undeniably real. I felt an unction to take this experience to the next level.

First, I made a sound. Then I made a few syllables. It sounded so unrefined, but I felt a shift happening. Choppy syllabic sounds started to string together into long-form babbles. I was dumbfounded. Words that sounded like an African language began pouring out of my mouth.

This point was when I fell to my knees under the weight of God's glory. I was overcome with pulsing energy, too strong for my body to stand up to. I was speaking in tongues—now starting to sound Arabic in nature. Tears streaming down my face, I bowed my head to the ground in reverence.

God was here.

God was encountering me.

God was baptizing me.

This was really happening.

For the following 30 minutes, I spoke in a completely foreign language, and I didn't stop. Intermittently, I would stop to praise and thank God in English for the experience that He was giving me. I had my face tucked into my hands, overcome by God's power. Warm, grateful tears dripped from my eyes and traveled down my hands to meet the floor. I kept praying in tongues until I felt His physical presence begin to subside.

Since that day, no person can tell me that God is not real. I had a true, undeniable encounter with the Spirit of God. Since then, I've operated in a greater level of faith, knowing that I have full confidence that there is a true force on the other side of my belief. Because I had been immersed in God's glory, I was also immersed with spiritual power. When you've encountered God firsthand, you operate in greater anointing and authority.

While the Bible isn't clear about WHY we're supposed to be baptized in the Spirit, it *is* straight-forward that we're supposed to be baptized. I've noticed some key differences in my spiritual development since this encounter. First, I've been able to discern the presence of God at a higher level. I tend to feel His presence as heat, warmth, and energy. Second, I am more confident in operating in my other spiritual gifts, having been able to speak in tongues (which in my opinion takes the most confidence to do). Lastly, I've had the privilege of being present in the baptism of other believers. I have helped to guide many people through the Holy Spirit baptism. All of these things bring me closer to God and have had an immense impact of my spiritual development.

Understand that every baptism of the Holy Spirit manifests differently. Not everyone will feel *heat*. Not everyone will speak in *tongues*. Not everyone will feel overcome by *emotion*. This is *my* account of how the Spirit encountered *ME*. Speaking in tongues is *not* the same as being baptized in the Holy Spirit; speaking in tongues is simply one of the potential pieces of evidence that you have been baptized. Other evidence includes worship, activating other spiritual gifts, and prophesying. Do not pursue the baptism of the Holy Spirit in order to speak in tongues. That's not the prize. Pursue to the baptism of the Holy Spirit out of obedience. Because scripture directs us to do it, we should do it. Whatever experience God decides to give you, receive it with gladness.

If you're looking at learning more about how the baptism of the Holy Spirit practically works, reference and study these scriptures:

Matthew 3:11 (What did John the Baptism promise Jesus would do?)

Acts 11:15-17 (How did Peter describe the Gentiles' encounter with the Holy Spirit?

Luke 24:49; Acts 1:4-5 (What did Jesus tell his disciples they were to do after he ascended to heaven?)

Acts 2:1-6; Acts 8:14-19; Acts 9:17-19; Acts 10:44-48; Acts 19:1-6 (How did these people receive the Spirit? Describe what happened in each account)

Luke 11:13 (Who does the Father give the Holy Spirit to?)

PRACTICE YOUR GIFTS

God wants to use you. This is why He has equipped you with spiritual gifts. Spiritual gifts are not for you—they're for the benefit of others. We owe it to others to get good at our gifts. We need to refine, sharpen, and strengthen our ability to operate in our gifts effectively and confidently. Competence builds confidence and practice makes perfect. The secret ingredient to supercharge your Develop stage is to *practice your spiritual gifts.*

You can't practice your gifts if you don't know your gifts. **Romans 12:6–8, 1 Corinthians 12:8–10, 1 Corinthians 12:28–30, Ephesians 4:11, 1 Peter 4:11** all provide lists of some of the spiritual gifts that are available to us as believers. In the same way that no two personalities are alike, no two people have the same set of gifts. There is no limit on how many spiritual gifts God can give you.

Some spiritual gifts include:

Prophecy, Serving, Teaching, Exhortation, Giving, Leadership, Mercy, Word of wisdom, Word of knowledge, Faith, Gifts of healing, Miracles, Distinguishing between spirits, Tongues, Interpretation of tongues, Kinds of healings, Helps, Administration, Speaking, and Rendering service

Are you admin-savvy? Are you a great teacher? Are you helpful? Do you have the ability to perform miracles? Of this spiritual gifts list, identify which of these gifts you operate in. Also ask the Holy Spirit which gifts are inside of you that you've been allowing to lay dormant. Once your gifts are identified, take them seriously. In the same way that a professional would commit to refining their corporate craft, every Christian should commit to refining their spiritual gifts.

When it comes to spiritual gifts, there are no "haves" and "have-nots." While some people may be more gifted than others, God will judge whether or not each person is stewarding their gifts and multiplying their gifts based on their potential. A gift buried in the ground—no matter how great of a measure it was given to the person—will never be more powerful than a gift put to work and multiplied.

Every gift requires practice in order to be refined. This even includes the more "spiritual" gifts, such as prophecy, healing, and miracles. It is often that we give grace for those who are gifted to help, teach, and give, but expect those who speak in tongues and distinguish between Spirits to be ready-made. Whether seemingly more-spiritual or more-practical, the gift must be put to the test in order to grow. Every single gift requires diligence, attention, practice, and refinement.

Whenever God told me that I was anointed to prophesy, I practiced it listening to the voice of God. I then gave prophetic words to my friend Jada. Most words were accurate, but I gave one inaccurate prophetic word that I'll never forget. I told her that her next child would be a girl, and that her name would be "Lily." She didn't fully resonate with that prophetic word, believing that her next child would be a son. Soon after that, while I was pregnant and we were searching for baby girl names, my husband and I fell in love with the name *Lily* for our daughter. What I thought God was speaking for *her* He was speaking for *me*. While Jada did go on to have a girl, I learned a valuable lesson about prophecy— there is room for error!

There is room for error with *every* spiritual gift. This is where the importance of the *Develop* stage comes into play. Many people want greater influence, bigger crowds, and a brighter spotlight. What they fail to realize is that the spotlight not only illuminates your strengths, but it also exposes your weaknesses. For this reason, you should never desire to rush your season of development. This season is paired with obscurity—the privilege of practicing without the pressure of being seen. If you're called to teach and you misquote a scripture to a friend from church, they'll cut you some slack. If you misquote a scripture at a small group of 8 women, you might have to apologize, but everyone will move on. However, if you misquote a scripture while preaching at a conference of 5,000... well, that's a big problem. The scripture says, "Dear brothers and sisters, not many of you should become teachers in the church, for we who teach will be judged more strictly." This scripture is essentially asserting that titles come with added pressure, accountability, and responsibility, so don't rush into a place you haven't developed into yet. Developing in private is not a punishment, it's a *privilege*. So practice in private so that when you're in public, you operate in power and not in *potential*.

STAGE FOUR

CHANGE

LET'S PLAY PRETEND

Brittany and I stood outside on my backyard porch under the scorching summer heat in Fort Worth, Texas. Brittany was my best friend. She held that title for as long as I could remember. I was the leader, because I was a month older and strong-willed. She was the pretty one, because her mom always dressed her in the cutest clothes and most adorable hair barrettes. There were few days that we hadn't spent together. We did everything together. Our skin was sun-kissed from the countless times we had slid down our slip n' slide, swam in our blow-up pool, played hopscotch on the concrete, and played pretend outside that summer.

"Let's say how we will be when we're 16," Brittany suggested.

I liked the thought of this. We were about nine years old at the time. Who would *older Amanda* be? We began visualizing our looks.

"I'll have long, dark wavy hair and I'll have pretty clothes." I said.

"I'll have long, straight black hair. I'll wear heels and a mini skirt." Brittany said.

I was surprised that she was confident enough to know that heels would go with a mini skirt, and that she'd look good in that ensemble when she's 16. But then again, her mom looked like a movie star just about every time I saw her. I rarely saw her mom without heels and lipstick. She carried a glory cloud of expensive perfume everywhere she went. My mom was made for cuddles, baking cookies, driving me to choir, and gardening. Brittany's mom was made for makeup, nail painting, choosing outfits and shopping trips. Those things were all things that intrigued me, yet they were so foreign to me.

"I'll drive a convertible with the top down, and I'll have a cute, tall boyfriend," Brittany continued.

I felt so behind. How did she know which car she'd have? How was she so sure that a cute, tall boy would be interested in her? I was so shy around the boys at school. Would there ever be a boy who found me beautiful and interesting? Would that be my reality? Is that what I wanted, too? I continued to consider my image. It was hard for me to muster up an outer style; it was something that I didn't have experience in.

Brittany continued on about how she'd be cool and popular, and how she'd have all of the right things to deem her as an "it girl." I never believed that I had what it took to be that. My mom wasn't a popular or fashionable woman herself. She told me stories of growing up on a farm, staying out of the spotlight, and avoiding shopping trips. While I had a burning desire to be a "girly girl," my only maternal example was nothing like that. And my dad wasn't a fan of when I painted my nails or played in makeup with Brittany.

I knew I wanted to have my own identity, both inwardly and outwardly, yet I struggled to believe that I'd ever rise to the level of outward beauty that I saw in other teen girls. They seemed so untouchable to me. Would I ever be a cool girl? Would I ever be a pretty girl? Would people ever notice me? I doubted that I would ever know the right things to say around others, the right things to wear around others, or the right things to do to be accepted. I focused on what I *did* believe about myself. I left those thoughts behind to start visualizing what I'd grow up to accomplish.

"I'll grow up to be a singer," I said. I had always wanted to pursue music. I had spent at least eight hours a week in choir rehearsals. I had tried dance, tae kwon do, and even gymnastics; but the only thing that really stuck with me and my parents was when I did music. They always told me I could go far with it.

"I'll be a dancer!" Brittany said. She was always a natural at dancing. "Are you going to be a pop star?"

"I think I'll be a Christian singer." I replied. I had known God from a very young age. I couldn't think back to a time when I didn't feel close to God.

"I'll also be a writer," I said. I had always loved writing. My parents always told me that I was great at writing, and so did my teachers. I dreamt of writing novels and kids' books. I visualized traveling the world as a best-selling author. Whether or not I would grow up to be a looker, I hoped that people would love hearing what I had to say.

I trusted that I would have power, but I wondered if some of my deepest desires would be met. I believed that I could be the president someday, but I wasn't sure if I'd find love. I believed that I would be skilled and talented, but I questioned whether I'd fit in. I knew that I was smart, but I wasn't sure if I'd ever be beautiful.

I was so impressionable at this age. It was the age right before puberty, when most girls start to take into account how they measure up to the kids at school. I noticed the world around me in a new way. Where I used to only care about what my teachers at school and leaders at church thought about me, I suddenly began to care about if the girls in school would accept me, and if boys would ever want me.

I felt as if I needed to start considering who I was becoming. Who I wanted to be was thin, beautiful, stylish, and attractive. I was a short, chubby, frizzy-headed smart girl who wore lopsided glasses. While I wanted to be beautiful like Brittany, I wasn't sure if I could ever be anything different. This was the time in my life where I started to question my purpose and my calling. My call hinged upon my image, and I was already measuring up short. I wasn't one of those girls who was told she was pretty before she was smart; I was bred to believe that I was strong, tough, resilient, and sharp. I just didn't grasp beauty. I didn't grasp acceptance. I wasn't sure if I would ever find fulfillment in life without beauty, admiration and love. I didn't want to grow up to be smart and strong without being pretty and desired. While I effortlessly believed that I would be somebody, I wondered if that somebody would be beautiful enough. Skinny enough. Cherished enough. Wanted enough. This is when I began internalizing shame about who I was, thinking that my identity was built on my ability to be beautiful and accepted—something that I just knew I wasn't.

As I finished visualizing with Brittany, I grabbed ahold of the older me that I conjured up. She was beautiful. She was smart. She was desirable. She was accepted. She was influential. She was a leader. She was kind. She was loved. She was infectious. She was happy. People noticed her. She had great friendships. She had skills and talents. She carried authority. Could I become her?

I see now that the Holy Spirit was showing me who I would become. That back-porch visualization with my childhood best friend on a hot, summer day was my first glimpse. The Spirit of God was showing me who I could be if I trusted Him; who I would become if I just believed. I was casting vision to the future, prophetically activating my best-self. I desired only what God desired for me: power, influence, authority, and a strong sense of self-love. The Spirit was showing me that I was made for more than questioning my worth, value, and beauty. He was whispering to me, "You'll love yourself one day. Your deepest desires will manifest. You'll be proud of who you become. You'll make an impact. You don't have to have it all or know it all right now. Just trust in Me."

THE VOICE OF DECEPTION

We all grow up wanting to make something of ourselves. When we're daydreaming little girls, none of us think to ourselves, "I want to grow up to be insecure and purposeless." However, for most of us, deception and doubt crept in somewhere along the way. You may have been told to smile and look cute. Maybe you were told you were just a pretty face. Perhaps your voice was stifled while your body was praised. Maybe you saw the world through the eyes of rejection. Everyone who you thought you could depend on left you wondering what you did wrong. Whatever your story is, take a moment to remember it. When was the first time what you didn't feel good enough, and why?

The enemy plants seeds of deception into young girls in attempts for those seeds to grow into a forest of doubt, disbelief and defeat as they mature into womanhood. Satan wants women walking around cowering, shrinking, doubting, second-guessing, and worrying. He wants to ensure that any success in our lives will be tainted with suggestion. He'll suggest,

"Are you *really* successful if you're fat?"

"Are you *sure* you're good enough if you're still single?"

"Are you *positive* that you're worthy is someone else is further along?"

From the beginning of time, the enemy has been a deceiver. He does not have *authority* over us, but he has the *power* of deception. The only authority he has is the authority we choose to yield to him. Knowing that he is without authority, his tactic is to use the power of his deception trick us into trading in our authority for the mirage of something better. He is particularly invested in the deception and downfall of women. Since the very beginning, he deceived Eve with the mirage of a better life that was available to her if she would just disobey God. Let's visit Genesis chapter 3 to unpack how this began:

"The serpent was the shrewdest of all the wild animals the Lord God had made. One day he asked the woman, 'Did God really say you must not eat the fruit from any of the trees in the garden?'" (vs. 1)

We see from the start of this chapter that the enemy's scheme was to deceive. When first engaging Eve, he doesn't explicitly lie to her—he *questions* her. These suggestive questions cause her doubt and second-guess what she knew to be true. She knew that God was protector. She knew that God was her provider. However, whenever the enemy asked, "Did God *really* say you must not eat the fruit from any of the trees in the garden?" the thought of questioning God was introduced. His first question polarized the truth—notice that the enemy asks Eve if God told her she couldn't eat from *any* of the trees.

Eve responded with what she knew: "'Of course we may eat fruit from the trees in the garden,' the woman replied.

'It's only the fruit from the tree in the middle of the garden that we are not allowed to eat. God said, 'You must not eat it or even touch it; if you do, you will die. '"

The enemy's first question insinuated that God was restricting *all* fruit from the trees in the garden from her. The truth was that God told Eve that she could freely eat from *any* tree in the garden *except* for one. This suggestion led to deception.

This is the same stealthy strategy that the enemy uses on women to date. While God may have given you access to the promise of salvation, forever relationship with Christ and forgiveness of sin, the enemy will suggest that God is withholding from you. You'll think God is keeping His love from you. You'll wonder if God is hiding His promises from you. You'll assume God is hoarding blessings and favor from you.

You'll strive to work for God religiously because you don't think relationship alone has saved you. Rather than resting in the Father's love, you'll start to believe that God is eager to punish you for all of your own mistakes and failures. You rehearse your shortcomings over and over and over again until they disguise themselves as the voice of love and protection. Rather than receiving God's forgiveness with gladness, you punish and sabotage yourself because you think you're beating God to the punch.

The enemy will *suggest* that you deserve less than God's best for your life. He will twist words and distort situations and pull on your emotions until you no longer rest on the sacrifice of Jesus Christ, and you begin to rely on the fragility of your flesh. You'll work and work and work, but to no avail. You'll still see your humanity. You'll still find that you fall short. And because your flesh fails, you'll think you're a failure. When you make a mistake, you'll think that *you're* a mistake. Through Jesus Christ, God has given you all of the promises of life, yet you'll think that there was more that He withheld from you because you weren't enough.

Does this sound like you? It can sometimes feel as if the enemy's voice is louder than God's voice. It can seem as if the lie seems truer than the truth. But the truth is that the enemy does not have the authority to rule your life. He cannot determine the thoughts that you think and he cannot make you feel the way that you feel. You've simply given him power to deceive you by giving him room to speak to you. Stop giving the enemy access to your mind! Stop giving the deceiver access to your heart! If you're ready to break the cycle, the good news is that you can change. Let's revisit Eve's encounter with the serpent in verse 4.

"You won't die!" the serpent replied to the woman. "God knows that your eyes will be opened as soon as you eat it, and you will be like God, knowing both good and evil."

The enemy shifts from a small suggestion to a blatant lie. Adam and Eve *had* the knowledge of good and evil. They knew that obeying God was *good* and that eating the forbidden fruit was *evil*. They simply didn't have experiential knowledge of good and evil. Up until that point, they lived sin-free lives. The enemy lied to them, making them think that God's warning wasn't for their good.

It's like when a parent tells a child that the stove is hot and that it's wrong to touch it; if they touch the stove they are going to get burned. That child obtains the *informational* knowledge of right and wrong and the consequences that come with choosing to disobey. However, when the child fails to trust the informational knowledge of the parent, they take matters into their own hands—they touch the stove. When they realize that the stove is hot and cry when they get burned, they obtain *experiential* knowledge.

Have you ever heard the enemy straight-up lie to you? Has the enemy ever dangled the carrot of prestige in front of your face, telling you that if you obtain it, then you'll feel worthwhile? Maybe you've heard the enemy lie to you and tell you that if you work hard enough for others, then you'll find acceptance and fulfillment. Perhaps the enemy has told you that God wants you to miss out on the better things in life, and that life is better when you sleep with that person or pop the pill. Instead of trusting what you know to be true, you take matters into your own hands. Rather than trusting that living under God's parameters is for your protection, you test the boundaries. You don't heed wisdom because you don't trust God. Like Adam and Eve, you have to touch the stove and get burned to know it's hot.

Here's the danger of giving the enemy the power to tell us lies: you'll believe them. Rather than exploring the depths of God's presence for gratification and fulfillment, you'll search for the presence of a man or woman to fulfill you. Instead of listening to the affirmation of God the Father, you'll look to the world to qualify and verify you. In lieu of pleading the blood of Jesus over your life, you'll attempt to be perfect all by yourself. Whenever you come into agreement with the suggestions that the enemy makes, you think God is holding out on you. You think you're missing something. You think, "there *has* be more."

YOU HAVE ALL YOU NEED

I know that back when I was visualizing my future with Brittany, I thought that there was more. I thought that being skinny would be the "more." Then, in college when I lost 50 pounds and weighed 98 pounds and wore a size 0, I found that skinny didn't fill the void in my heart. I thought that being accepted by other girls would be the "more." Then, when I joined a sorority and still felt lonely and othered, I found that acceptance only gets you so far without accepting yourself. I thought that finding the man of my dreams would be the "more." Then, when I married the perfect man of my dreams and I still felt insecure and inadequate, I realized that another human cannot fill the place of God in my life.

Don't be like me. Don't be like Eve. Trust that your life with God is *better* than life apart from Him. Trust that His parameters and boundaries are to protect you and give you a *good* future, not to withhold from you or shortchange you. Trust when He tells you,

> *Don't touch the stove.*
>
> *Don't touch that man.*
>
> *Don't apply for that job.*
>
> *Don't drink that liquor.*
>
> *Don't go to that website.*
>
> *Don't strive towards that goal.*
>
> *Don't look for acceptance in those people.*

God's don'ts are filled with grace. God's warnings are filled with love. God's wisdom is filled with protection.

Whenever I was playing pretend with Brittany in our backyard at nine years old, God showed me a glimpse of who I was. I was called to be a giant in the Spirit. A woman who champions women. A woman who is beautiful and confident.

A woman who doesn't back down. The moment that the enemy saw that God had a plan for my life, he was threatened. He knew that if I believed that I could become a powerful and secure woman, I would raise a powerful and secure daughter. He knew that if I could feel beautiful and significant while serving the Lord, that I would help other women do the same. The enemy was threatened. If I believed that I could be all that God called me to be, then I was a threat to the kingdom of darkness.

Now, this isn't about me. I'm sure that God has shown you glimpses of *your* kingdom identity, too. Satan wants to do everything in his power to keep you from showing up as her. The enemy understands that he doesn't have the authority to stop the plan of God manifesting in your life; he only has the power of deception. In the process of change—becoming the woman God destined you to be—know that God is not withholding from you. Do not feed into the voice of deception. As you pursue your purpose and work out your calling, you're inevitably going to make a huge splash in the world. The enemy will try to stop you by suggesting that there are no ripples, or that your splash wasn't big enough. Know this truth: you're a threat to the kingdom of darkness. You're making an impact, and God is withholding no good thing from you. Keep fighting. Keep pushing. Keep becoming.

I HAVE ARRIVED

I didn't come from much. I grew up in a neighborhood where I wasn't sure whether I was hearing illegal fireworks or gunshots. The people living across the street had cigarette butts embedded in their lawn, and they were always asking for money. My parents worked as employees outside of the home for 90% of their life. Work life was never intertwined with faith life, and was certainly not intertwined with family time. Not only that, but when I got into the college of my dreams, I spiraled out of control. I did all of the things that I shouldn't have done: drank underage, smoked illegally, cheated on my boyfriend, and denied my Christian faith.

Then, after God captured my heart, my whole life changed. I shed off the alcohol, sex, and cursing. I started reading the bible, praying, and rebuilding my life with Christ. Soon, a good, godly man found me valuable enough to marry, and we got married. We had an amazingly happy marriage and pursued God in everything that we did. Then, God called us to move to the city of Atlanta on *faith*. After serving at the church we were called to, my husband got ordained. Then we began pastoring a campus of that church at the same time that we stepped out into full-time entrepreneurship.

Now, my faith is completely intertwined with my work life. Almost weekly, I get to take women from my church out to coffee and pastor them. I get to mentor women, nationally and internationally. I get to work for myself from the comfort of my home. I'm writing this sentence from my bed. Now I make an income that is disproportionately greater than those in the zip code that I was raised in. Now I've built a community of thousands on social media of people who listen to my words and follow along with my life. I preach at my church, preach online, and have even been invited to travel and speak.

While I'm not a millionaire, I've had the taste of being able to pay for things that I used to think I didn't deserve. While I'm not famous, I've had the taste of dedicated social media followers singing my praises and fan-girling when they bump into me in public. While I'm still obligated to work, as an entrepreneur, I've had the taste of being able to sleep in as long as I'd like, take midday naps, and stay up late. I've been able to write a big check to support my family as missionaries. I've been able to be present to women, and those women profess that I've changed their lives. I've been invited to speak by popular and influential people. I've had the opportunity to schedule a last-minute vacation on a whim.

For my former self, the life that I live today—a flexible schedule, fulfilling work, small-scale fame, and financial increase—is a life of arrival. Yet... I haven't arrived. I never imagined that my life would look this way, and part of that scares me. I'm unsettled because I used to think that influence, income, and impact were all that you needed to be satisfied with life, but they're not. If my social media following, bank account, and level of impact I make on the lives of others scaled by ten times, I still wouldn't arrive. I still would have room to develop. I still would be working to extract "more."

I have to tell you the truth: even if the grass is greener on the other side, even if you got to the other side, that green grass won't satisfy you. If you're insecure at 200 followers, and then you'll still feel insecure at 2,000 followers, with 20,000 followers, 200,000 followers and 2,000,000 followers. If you are greedy and insatiable at $500 a month, then you'll likely be greedy and insatiable at $500 a week, $500 a day, $500 an hour, $500 a minute, and $500 a second. Even when it comes to the impact you make in the lives of others in your workplace, ministry, or personal life, there are 7,700,000,000 (that's BILLION) people that live on earth, and that number grows every single day. There will always be more lives to reach and people to impact.

If you think that influence, impact, or income will complete you, I'm here to tell you *that's a lie*. If you assume that knowledge, information, and intellect will complete you, I'm here to tell you *that's a lie*. Even if you believe that affirmations, positivity, and self-love will complete you, I'm here to tell you *that's a lie*. God is not finished with you now, and God will not be finished with you when you get "there." Life on earth has no arrival. Change is an ongoing sanctification process of belonging to God, shedding who you're not, developing in who you are, and expanding your capacity.

GROW YOUR CAPACITY MUSCLE

There's a popular Christianese saying that goes, "God won't ever put more on you than you can bear." I hear this phrase all. the. time. We assume that this *saying* is *scripture*, but it's not. When people say this catchphrase, they're actually thinking of 1 Cor. 10:13 that says, "And God is faithful; he will not let you be tempted beyond what you can bear. But when you are tempted, he will also provide a way out so that you can endure it." God won't allow you to be tempted beyond your capacity, but when you're in a season of development, He will often stretch you beyond your capacity. This stretching makes room for you to grow.

Consider the human body. Muscle is built on your body through muscle tension, muscle damage, and metabolic stress. Muscle growth requires a level of stress greater than what your body is used to. In order to apply stress your muscles, you simply lift heavier weights than what you're adapted to. If you've ever felt sore after a workout, what you're feeling is muscle damage from working out. This damage causes your body to release inflammatory molecules and immune system cells that activate cells to repair the damaged muscle. After you get rest and nutrition, your muscles are fueled to regenerate and grow.

This concept is also how we develop in life. Notice that it isn't the peachy times and sunny days that endow you with tough skin, grit, and perseverance. It's when you make it through being overwhelmed and being pressed on all sides that you grow strong and resilient. Because of the misconception that "God won't put more on you than you can bear," many Christians think it's strange when hard times come their way. They may assume that the enemy is up to something because they're suffering. However, 1 Peter 4:12 says,

> *Dear friends, don't be surprised at the fiery trials you are going through, as if something strange were happening to you. Instead, be very glad—for these trials make you partners with Christ in his suffering, so that you will have the wonderful joy of seeing his glory when it is revealed to all the world.*

Giving your life to God does not guarantee immediate health, wealth, and prosperity. While God loves to bless His children and give us good gifts, understand that there is a sanctification process that takes place that sets you on pace to your calling. You might think that if you jump, God will always catch you. In actuality, sometimes God will let you hit the ground just to prove to you that the ground won't kill you. He wants you to know that the boogeyman isn't real. You're tough. You're strong. You'll make it through.

Character is complementary to capacity. Character is like your core and capacity is like your arms. You may want to only focus on building your arm strength, but if your core is weak, you won't be able to do push-ups, pull-ups, or the bench press. Why is this? Because push-ups, pull-ups and bench presses all require your core muscles. You may be able to curl light weight using just your biceps, but the heavier weight you lift, the more core strength is required of you. As you add more weight on to your dumbbells, if your core is underdeveloped, you will eventually hit a threshold of weight that your core cannot withstand. This is how character and capacity coincide: If you try to develop in your capacity (the use of your abilities, skills, and gifts) without developing your character (your integrity), eventually you'll hit a threshold of capacity that your character cannot withstand.

In short, God doesn't want your character to fail under the weight of your capacity. God wants you to have strong biceps *and* a strong core. He wants you to have a high-level character paired with a high-level capacity. This is why God will *absolutely* place more weight on you than you can bear. You'll fight battles in private that challenge you. You'll get into relationships with people who hurt you. You'll be pushed to lift a weight that seems too heavy for you. This development will certainly make you sore for a time. But after your spiritual muscle is restored, you emerge more powerful, more authoritative, and more effective.

DON'T CRASH AND BURN

My husband and I have been speaking and teaching on healthy relationships and marriage for over six years now. We've always been advocates for healthy, happy, and holy covenants. For years, we've filmed videos about how to have a successful Christian relationship and transition into a godly marriage. We even wrote a book called, "Love Your First Year of Marriage." We were the couple who said things like, "marriage doesn't have to be hard!" We've counseled many couples, premaritally and in marriage, and helped people iron out wrinkles in their love life.

I'm not exactly sure how we managed to do all of that without regular dates. In our first two years of marriage, we didn't have kids, so we figured that we were "fine." We see each other a bunch, anyway, right?

Then, once we had our first child, we used the excuse, "well, he's young, and it's hard to find and pay for a babysitter."

Then, I got pregnant with our daughter. After I gave birth, things got complicated.

For the first time, our marriage got hard. For months. Right after my daughter was born, our marriage took a huge hit. We started having long, drawn-out emotional conversations nearly every day. Sometimes, we'd lose sleep staying up talking through our issues. How did we miss these things for so long? Having two kids to care for, a business to run, and a church to run, it was mentally, emotionally, and financially devastating. We burned out.

My passion for life was fizzling out. It was hard for me to maintain my friendships, love others well, be patient with my kids, and love myself. I even hit a rock-bottom night where I cut myself with a razor, having been overcome with feelings of hopelessness. I'm not proud of it, being a woman who leads other women, but it happened. I felt like my world was too heavy to bear, and God wasn't there to spot me. I was walking around with mental fog and was severely sleep deprived. My marriage was always my safe place, but during these months, it was just *hard*.

After all of our talks, it took us about two months to get our footing back under us. After we got our bearings, it was then when we realized *why* we hit this marital low. We were working on our church, working on our business, and raising our children all without rest or enjoyment. We figured that since we were working together, it qualified as quality time, when it didn't. We thought we knew one another, but we didn't fully. We were simply making assumptions about one another based on our observation, but not based on authentic conversation. We burned out in marriage because we didn't set aside time to date one another.

We have regular date days every single Tuesday now. This is the time when we aren't required to work and we can simply be romantic. We focus on enjoyment and *not* on productivity. We've gone on more dates in the first six months of 2019 than we have in the entire first five years of our marriage. After we've implemented regular date days, our marriage has flipped upside right. It's stronger than ever before.

Not only are we a healthier couple, but we're also a happier couple. We have better sex, more stimulating conversations, and more bonding experiences together. We used to think "we can't afford to have regular date days," and now we think, "we can't afford NOT to have regular date days." We thought that we would be a "power couple" if we could skip through dates and just build together, but we were wrong. We're far more powerful and productive after we invest time into rest, relaxation and enjoyment. This builds us up more than anything else.

Now, the same goes for your walk with Christ. The secret sauce to developing in your capacity at a quick rate is taking adequate rest. Muscles cannot grow without adequate rest and nutrition. In the same way that spanking your children without also teaching them is abuse, working under pressure without giving yourself time to rest is abuse, too. You become healthy and strong by exercising six days a week and resting on the seventh. You become destructive and detrimental by exercising every day, never giving your muscles a chance to regenerate or rejuvenate. Without rest, pain makes you weaker. With rest, pain makes you stronger.

God did not design us to work without rest. God did not plan for us to undergo stress without ever experiencing relief. God made the world in six days and then He rested on the seventh. He didn't have to do this. He is God. He is omnipotent. Scripture says that He doesn't faint or grow weary. However, God was setting the example for how we are to develop mentally, spiritually, emotionally, and physically. He was showing us that in order to become like Him, we need rest.

Practically, while you're developing in capacity, what does rest look like? Start taking breaks. Schedule in a day a week that you're not going to focus on productivity. Don't think about your work obligations, family obligations, church obligations, or time obligations. Schedule a time in your calendar that says, "Time to do nothing." So, when obligation knocks on your door to try and squash your time of rest, tell obligation, "I'm sorry, I'm already booked for that time."

During this time of rest, focus on intimacy with God and enjoyment of life. God doesn't want you to work through life without ever having the chance to sit back and enjoy the fruit of your labor. King Solomon shares his perspective on this topic in the book of Ecclesiastes:

I have seen personally what is the only beneficial and appropriate course of action for people: to eat and drink, and find enjoyment in all their hard work on earth during the few days of their life which God has given them, for this is their reward.

King Solomon was asserting that there is reward in rest after work. This may be a new concept to you if you're a workaholic, or you take pride in being busy. No matter how challenging this may be, I'm telling you that it's essential. Don't expect to keep running without resting. Dedicate a day to taking a sabbath. Now, a sabbath is traditionally a day of religious observance and abstinence from work, kept by Jews from Friday evening to Saturday evening, and by most Christians on Sunday. However, you can decide to sabbath in whatever way and time builds enjoyment, fulfillment and rest into your schedule. Here are some ideas on how you can spend your time when you're not working: take a soak in the bath. Get your nails done. Watch a new movie. Go get a bite to eat with a friend. Go for a walk with good music. Journal and doodle. Try a new hobby that doesn't make you money. Take the focus away from your work and put the focus on your pleasure.

Place the spotlight on preventative self-care to spare you the pain of having to later have an intervention. Cultivating a healthy circle of friendships around you ensures that it won't get to that point. And if it does, you won't be alone. You need friends to be able to look you in your face and tell you, "you're not yourself," "you need to rest," or even a simple, "we need to hang out." This only comes about in your life if you're intentionally vulnerable about your everyday pressures before they become serious problems. If no one ever sees what your hurt looks like, they won't recognize it when you need them. Be proactive and preventative by building a strong support system of a few trusted people (2-3 is plenty) that you hold up and that hold you up.

IF YOU CRASH AND BURN

If you find that you've fallen into a pit of burnout or depression, then you owe it to yourself to slow down. There are key indicators that you've run yourself into the ground: Some people will become numb, and others will become cynical. You may stop believing the best, hoping for the best, or praying for the best. Others will partake in self-medicating and self-harming behaviors like drinking, smoking, sleeping around, taking pills, binge eating, excessing spending and shopping, spending hours on social media, cutting their body, and/or watching porn. Some people will quit what God told them to do. Some will even fantasize about quitting life all together. I know that I have been in that dark place before. But those who are wise will simply **slow down**. They'll decide to cut back a little bit instead of quitting all together. They will choose to take a breather—not to stop breathing.

Whenever my husband and I went through our rough patch after my daughter was born, I remember hearing the voice of the enemy try to tell me to give up. While our conversations were healthy, bringing about growth, and helping us make true progress, the enemy tried to negate that it was all worth the work. Why? Because I was tired. He tried to prey on my exhaustion to tempt me to give up all together. Was I tempted to leave my marriage? Not once. What I tempted to commit suicide? Not this time around. But I did check out of life for a few weeks. My productivity tanked and I wanted to stop working.

But I decided that I wouldn't stop. I kept putting one foot in front of the other and showing up every day. Every day made me 1% better than the day before. However, during this process of my own personal restoration, I grew frustrated with how long the process was taking. Whenever we would have another hard conversation, I felt so much shame. I would say things like,

"I should be further along than I am…"

"Why aren't I back to normal yet?"

"When will I feel myself?"

"When will I operate at 100% again?"

After all, I am a women's mentor. I am a pastor's wife. I have followers on Instagram that look up to me. What I didn't realize was that burnout takes time to recover from. If you've been going years without scheduling sabbaths, scheduling days for enjoyment (like date days in marriage), while simultaneously pouring out for others at church, in your friendships, at your job, and in your external endeavors, then after you crash, it's going to take time to regain your "new normal." So, slow down. Carve out time to think. Make time to pray. Give yourself time to cry. Schedule out time to walk. Allow yourself time to talk. Offer yourself time to process and heal.

Comparison will also rob you of your opportunity to rest and restore. My husband comes across to me as superman. He is tender yet tough, restful yet incredibly resilient. Much of the process of him and I getting back to 100% health in our marriage was not our relationship with one another; it was me. Just me. Oftentimes, I would feel shame that Michael was back in action and able to be productive and pastor effectively while it was still taking me time to restore. I compared myself to him, thinking that he was the model of Christian excellence, while I was failing miserably. But that wasn't the case. Understand that comparison while resting will tempt you to work to catch up. And work is the opposite of rest.

After I had my c-section for my second child, I wanted to get back into the groove of exercising immediately. I was eager to shed my pregnancy pounds to get back to my regular size 2 jeans. I compared myself to women who were snatching back and getting back into their fitness routine right after giving birth, neglecting to remember that I had a traumatic abdominal surgery, while the women I was comparing myself to had successful and uncomplicated vaginal deliveries. After injuring my hips from running three

miles after only five weeks postpartum, I learned my lesson.
I needed to stop comparing my recovery process to others'. I
needed to slow down.

JOIN ME IN PARADISE

I was walking with friends down a long, narrow, white hallway in a building. They were chatting, and life was going on as it normally would. I began to disassociate with the conversation. It didn't seem quite as important anymore. Suddenly, I could see beyond my surroundings.

I walked away from the group without them noticing. We were experiencing reality in two different dimensions. Being able to supernaturally see outside of the brick walls of our building, I pulled back the veil on their fantasy to expose reality. When I opened my eyes to the outside world, I saw nations at war with one another. The earth was plagued with catastrophe, marked by red and orange explosions. I heard the sound of destruction and despair fill my ears. The apocalyptic scene alarmed me. The world was ending.

Suddenly, I merged back into my company's reality. They didn't notice that I went missing. They kept joking and laughing as if the world weren't falling to pieces. Did they know their impending doom? I didn't ask any questions. I knew something that they didn't. I resolved to keep observing. We continued walking down the hallway.

As I walked, I came across a TV on my right. The imagery was so striking that I had to stop and watch. On the TV, there was a news anchorwoman and anchorman. The pair casually conversed with each other through polished, fake smiles. A *breaking news* picture appeared in the upper right-hand corner of the screen as alarming words in all caps rolled across the bottom. The catastrophes that I just saw a moment ago were now being broadcast across national television.

The anchors panned their video to a host in a different area standing in front of where an explosive catastrophe is happening. I saw pictures of angst, sorrow, and hopelessness. Homes, cities, villages, and families were being destroyed. The brave anchor shared her breaking news story about wars that were happening around the world. Filming her story in the midst of violence and turmoil, the host was committed to delivering her story at the expense of her own life. Why was she *working* instead of taking cover? It seemed to me like a vain way to die.

The Spirit led me away from the TV. I walked away from the group of friends, starting in the opposite direction of the hallway. I *had* to get away. I walked through the red brick wall of the building and entered into the outside world. Outside of the building, I was met with an enormous spherical orb. It was nearly the size of a small house. The vehicle looked rustic, ancient, and impenetrable. The door of the orb opened from the top, like butterfly-wing doors on a sports car. I had never seen anything like it.

From out of nowhere, hundreds of people entered into this huge vehicle. They seemed more like souls, being translucent in nature. I entered in, too. I knew that I was led away from the crowd because I was summoned to be here. After the doors shut, the orb transported us up in a steady upward motion. As I was being transported up, headed in the same direction as hundreds of other people, I questioned whether or not I was in the right place.

After a couple of minutes, we arrived in the clouds. The doors opened in the same butterfly fashion. It was undeniable—I had arrived in heaven. All the people who entered the vehicle with me traveled together on a narrow path headed toward a light. I wasn't supposed to go with them. It was at that moment that I realized that all of those people were the dead in Christ, and I wasn't dead. I was simply here to visit.

As the last person to find my way into heaven, I was welcomed with golden gates before me and clouds beneath my feet. In front of the gate stood a large, loving figure. I couldn't believe my eyes: I was standing face-to-face with Jesus. The very moment I saw Him, I knew that He was Jesus. My Spirit identified Him. I knew that He was my savior.

In the skies above Him, I saw a spectrum of colors unidentifiable to the natural human eye. I saw rainbows. I saw clouds. I saw a physical representation of joy, peace, and hospitality. I saw the wings of angels flying above Him, their wingspan shockingly wide. They were all celebrating in what felt like victory. I was greeted with the ringing symphony of all of heaven rejoicing; not just the angels, but everything in it. All that existed praised God. I had never experienced or seen anything like it before. After taking in the glorious introduction to heaven, again I laid eyes on my savior.

Jesus was the definition of light. He was the purest form of light that I had ever seen. His glorious, pure, white light radiated off of Him to illuminate all of heaven. When He turned His head, beams of gold flickered off of Him. His robes were white and heavy, masterfully lined white pure, celestial light and divine gold. I was in awe.

He communicated to my Spirit, not needing to open His mouth to speak. Extending His arms, He told me that all of heaven is mine.

"No, Jesus, no! I don't deserve this. Look at all I've done," I pleaded, pointing to earth. I was stuck in my sin and unrepentant during this time in my life. "I don't belong here. I don't deserve this." I said, desperately trying to convince Jesus.

Jesus calmly smiled at me and said, "It's ok. I love you."

I turned around to look at the earth beneath me. That's where all of the unsaved souls were. They were surrounded in darkness and blindness. Earth seemed so bleak and irrelevant now as I stood before the Prince of Peace. I pointed to earth and told Jesus that I deserved to be there. He wouldn't budge. We patiently waited as I pleaded and cried at His feet.

As I looked to Jesus, He was so calm and humbly confident. He smiled with complete sincerity and said, "You're forgiven. I don't remember. This is YOURS." It was my inheritance, it belonged to me.

I began thanking Jesus for giving me the greatest gift ever, a gift that I didn't deserve. It was at this moment that I finally understood the definition of grace. It was far beyond my wildest imagination, knowing that I was a wretched sinner yet being given a magnificent gift that I did nothing to earn or deserve. I erupted in praise. I endlessly thanked Jesus, knowing that there was nothing that I could possibly give Him.

Several times I asked Him, "Can I give you something? Is there something that I can do? Let me do something."

He was unshaken. He just kept comforting me.

Then, He opened his arms to hug me.

Without thought, I plunged into His arms and I squeezed Him with all my strengrh.

At this moment, I experienced true love. He is love personified. When He hugged me, He encompassed me in perfect love. This love was a physical force beyond my wildest imagination. The force oscillated in a magnetic circle, pulling me toward Him, uniting me with Jesus. I understood later that this force of love surrounding Jesus and I was the Holy Spirit binding us together in perfect unity. The Spirit was an all-encompassing, drenching, unbreakable presence. It was clear that there was no force greater or more powerful in all of the universe.

In that moment, I couldn't desire anything else. All of my wildest dreams—every little hurt—everything was mended. I couldn't think about anything else. Nothing else mattered.

The Spirit's love connected Jesus and I to a corner in heaven where another bright light was coming from. I knew that was where God the Father was. I was connecting with God the Father and Jesus. In that moment, we all were one.

THIS ISN'T THE END

This was my account of heaven. God gave me this dream in 2011 when I had given up on my Christian faith to pursue all that the world had to offer. I was recklessly pursuing sin and loving every bit of it. I didn't expect God to encounter me this way. God was low on my radar. In fact, I thought that He had forsaken me. I mean, I had forsaken Him, so shouldn't He have? After this Holy encounter, I *still* did not submit my life to God. The experience shook me to my core, yet I chose not surrender. As time progressed, I couldn't shake the dream. I couldn't shake that in my most rebellious phase of life, God pursued me. He kept pursuing me until I finally turned my life around and gave it back to Him.

You know what was most interesting about this dream? When I was on earth, earthly reality seemed like a dream while heaven felt so real. Before I woke up from my dream, this was the message that Christ left me with in heaven: you have to go back and tell others about Me. Life is but a vapor. I went on to record this encounter in a YouTube video to share with as many people as possible.

I share this encounter to shift your perspective from earth to heaven, and from present to eternity. It's easy to believe that this life is all that there is. That's why the temptation is so great to consume all of the delicacies and test all of the boundaries that the world has to offer. When you live as if earth is your home, you begin to believe that your own glory, freedom, comfort, gluttony, greed, perfectionism, and intellect will satisfy you. You strive to attain all that life can give you, as if you don't have an inheritance of peace, joy, and uncompromising love waiting for you on the other side.

Do you want true change? The truth is that while change is ongoing, you'll never arrive. While you're here on earth, wrapped in your body of flesh, you're in an ever-evolving process of *becoming*. Arrival is not a special moment of promotion at your job, the opportunity to speak on a big stage, achieving your goal weight, or paying off your debt. Arrival isn't attaining a certain measure of love, joy, peace, patience, kindness, goodness, gentleness, faithfulness or self-control. Arrival isn't when you hit a certain number of people prayed for, lives given to Jesus, or hours spent fasting. Arrival isn't even your moment of salvation, your baptism in water, or your baptism in the Holy Spirit. Our arrival point is when we meet Jesus face-to-face in heaven.

This is the moment when we are glorified. Our old bodies—made of dust—are done away with, and we're given our new, perfected bodies, fit for heaven. This is the moment. This is the time. This is the place. We are no longer becoming. In the blink of an eye, we simply *are*. Rather than living with the tension of the futility of our flesh, we flourish in the freedom of the perfection of our Spirit. We fully belong. We fully shed. We fully developed. We fully changed.

Read 1 Corinthians 15:42-58 to understand this truth:

> *It is the same way with the resurrection of the dead. Our earthly bodies are planted in the ground when we die, but they will be raised to live forever. Our bodies are buried in brokenness, but they will be raised in **glory**. They are buried in weakness, but they will be raised in strength. They are buried as natural human bodies, but they will be raised as **spiritual bodies**. For just as there are natural bodies, there are also spiritual bodies.*

The Scriptures tell us, "The first man, Adam, became a living person." But the last Adam—that is, Christ— is a life-giving Spirit. What comes first is the natural body, then the spiritual body comes later. Adam, the first man, was made from the dust of the earth, while Christ, the second man, came from heaven. Earthly people are like the earthly man, and heavenly people are like the heavenly man. Just as we are now like the earthly man, we will someday be like the heavenly man.

What I am saying, dear brothers and sisters, is that our **physical bodies cannot inherit the Kingdom of God.** *These dying bodies cannot inherit what will last forever.*

But let me reveal to you a wonderful secret. We will not all die, but we will all be **transformed!** *It will happen in a moment, in the blink of an eye, when the last trumpet is blown. For when the trumpet sounds, those who have died will be raised to live forever. And we who are living will also be transformed. For our dying bodies must be* **transformed** *into bodies that will never die; our mortal bodies must be* **transformed** *into immortal bodies.*

Then, when our dying bodies have been transformed into bodies that will never die, this Scripture will be fulfilled:

"Death is swallowed up in victory.
death, where is your victory?
O death, where is your sting?"

For sin is the sting that results in death, and the law gives sin its power. But thank God! He gives us victory over sin and death through our Lord Jesus Christ.

So, my dear brothers and sisters, be strong and immovable. Always work enthusiastically for the Lord, for you know that nothing you do for the Lord is ever useless.

This passage of scripture is making it plain for us: the true change — the monumental butterfly moment where we're made brand new — that takes place in heaven. Throughout this life, you'll feel the tension of your Spirit emerging as a butterfly from your early shell — your body. You'll feel the pain of your flesh not being "enough" while the Spirit within you is more than enough. You'll feel the frustration of your flesh failing while your Spirit is flying. This is why the cover of this book shows half of the butterfly trapped in its shell while the other half is fully-emerged; it will feel that way until Jesus comes back.

I love that this translation of scripture repeatedly uses the word "transform" to describe our miraculous glorification. The word *transform* is defined in the Miriam-Webster dictionary as, "to change in composition or structure; to change the outward form or appearance of; to change in character or condition; *convert*." At the core of transformation is change. And in this moment, we change in structure, having moved from physical bodies to spiritual ones. We change in outward appearance, having moved from the appearance of aging to death, to existing for eternity. We change from character and condition, having been built for sin, to being programmed for righteousness. This is our moment complete metamorphosis. This is our hope.

It's interesting that the word "convert" is the dictionary's go-to synonym for *transform*. We often refer to a *convert* as a person who was once lost that gives their life to follow Jesus. The day and place of the person's prayer of salvation or even their baptism is often celebrated and commemorated as the day of their conversion. But the truth is that the day we give our lives to Christ is our day of *salvation*, but the day that we meet Christ in heaven is our day of *conversion*—the day we're fully transformed for glory, *forever*.

The good news is that while our bodies are dead, our Spirit is alive in Christ. Romans 8:9-11 explains it this way:

> *You, however, are not in the realm of the flesh but are in the realm of the Spirit, if indeed the Spirit of God lives in you. And if anyone does not have the Spirit of Christ, they do not belong to Christ. But if Christ is in you, then even though your body is subject to death because of sin, the Spirit gives life because of righteousness. And if the Spirit of him who raised Jesus from the dead is living in you, he who raised Christ from the dead will also give life to your mortal bodies because of his Spirit who lives in you.*

It is the Spirit inside of you that is the fully-emerged butterfly! Where you fall short, when you're not enough, when you lose heart, God's Spirit inside of you is bursting at the seams, beaming with brilliance. His Spirit shows us glimpses of the beings we will be when everything else is wiped away, and all that is left is us, God, and this powerful force of love bonding us together. Your mission on earth is to surrender yourself— your desires, hopes, dreams, cares, thoughts, motivations...

everything—to the Spirit. The more surrendered your flesh is, the more striking your Spirit becomes. As you **belong** to God through Bible reading, prayer and worship, you *are* change. As you shed from the pain of your past and the desires of your flesh by engaging, healing and confessing in healthy community, you *are* change. As you develop in the gifts of the Spirit and become familiar with your higher self—the Spirit within you—you *are* change. As you follow in God's plan for your life and make disciples, you *are* change.

So there is good news and there is better news. The good news is that you don't have to wait for the moment that you meet Jesus to become. Right now, where you are, you can belong, shed, develop and change. The fulfillment of life isn't in the arrival; the reward is in the process. the reward is in the work. The reward is in the change. Rather than criticize yourself for how far along you think you should be, begin to celebrate the transformation that you're undergoing every single day.

The better news is that this life isn't the end. It's only the beginning. Your present trials, temptations, and transformations are *nothing* compared to the glory that will be revealed to you and through you. Every time that you worry that you're not measuring up, celebrate the fact that you're not supposed to yet. There will be a moment where every tear is wiped away from your eye, every frustration is eliminated, and all that is left is you and Jesus. That thing that once embarrassed you... it will become a distant memory. That imperfection that you see every day... it will be inconsequential. That thorn in your flesh that you can't seem to shake... it will cease to exist. You will be free from every burden, pain, trouble, and affliction. You will become fully alive to joy, peace, relief, and pure love. Every day, that moment is closer than before. Keep that vision in front of you. Don't focus your eye on the pain that was; focus you gaze on the hope that is to come.

CHANGE ACTION PLAN

First, the egg was laid. Then a caterpillar emerged. It grew and it shed. Then, it tucked into its pupa. Within it, the caterpillar developed and transformed into a seemingly-new creature. Then, it is finally time for the butterfly's debut. When the butterfly first emerges, both of the wings are soft and folded against its body. Once the butterfly has rested after emerging, it pumps blood into the wings in order to get them moving and flapping. This is when the butterfly will fly and ultimately reproduce.

The final stage of The Life Cycle of Change is... CHANGE. Change is not a place of arrival; it is a place of work. While speaking Christanese, a common phrase we say is that we want to, "reap a harvest." The funny thing is, if you know anything about farming, or if you can google, you'll learn that the harvest season is the most labor-intensive time of the agricultural cycle. Harvesting requires you to collect all that has been grown so that it can be put to use. So if you are approaching *Change*, understand that change takes work.

This is the time when you stay in constant development as you develop others, reproducing yourself in every sphere that you fly in and out of. You have no boundaries; the possibilities are endless. Your responsibility holds true:

LET GO OF THE LIE

Where are some areas in your life that you've allowed the enemy to assert his suggestions and lies? What did the enemy bait you with? Whether it was the need for control, security, success, significance, escape, acceptance, knowledge, value, perfection or whatever else, you don't have to go around God to get it. God isn't holding out on you. Rather than make the same mistake that Eve did, don't listen to the voice of the enemy. Don't touch the stove. Anything that you could potentially pursue without God can burn you. Don't pursue experiential knowledge when God has already given you the informational knowledge that *the stove is hot*.

Visualize the woman that God has called you to be. What does she look like? How does she hold herself? What are her values? What does she know to be true? What are her friends like? Who is she connected to? What is she concerned with? What problems does she solve? What type of people does she reach? What impact is she making for God? Why is she a threat to the enemy? What will she accomplish that will rival the kingdom of darkness? Once you have that picture in your head, then start showing up as her.

REPRODUCE

I know, I know.

After all of your time spent in prayer in worship...

After all of the scriptures you've learned and mastered...

After every heartache that you've confronted...

After every person you've forgiven...

After every skill you've cultivated...

After every gift that you've mastered...

After all of the lies you've denounced...

And after all of the loads that you've carried...

You want to shine. No one else should take your glory. No one else deserves the spotlight. But I have to tell you the truth: change isn't just for you. Change is for your sister. Change is for your son. Change is for your daughter. Change is for your church. Change is for your workplace.

Change is for your nation. You aren't fulfilling your destiny without birthing new destiny into the lives of others.

We all admire Billy Graham, but no one acknowledges the person who preached to Billy Graham. People look up to my husband as a pastor, but no one ever inquires about the one man who discipled him in college. Women thank me for leading them and guiding them, but no one ever thanks Robbie or Christina—the two individuals who led me back to Christ in college. You don't need to be the most known, recognized, or seen in order to make a change.

2 Peter 3:9 says, "The Lord is not slow in keeping his promise, as some understand slowness. Instead he is patient with you, not wanting anyone to perish, but everyone to come to repentance." This means that God is patiently waiting for everyone to be saved. He doesn't want any one person to go to hell, spend eternity away from Him, or live a purposeless, meaningless life. He is patiently waiting for you to step up to the plate to find the people who need rescue. Do you remember the person who reached out to you? If you ever feel indebted to that person when you remember them, know that the best way to repay them for the way they reproduced new life within you is to reproduce new life in the lives of others.

Find at least one person who needs what you can give them. Don't feel threatened or tempted by their potential, and don't overlook their potential or disqualify them before your pursuit; simply give. Remember that the passage in 1 Corinthians ends by saying, *"So, my dear brothers and sisters, be strong and immovable. Always work enthusiastically for the Lord, for you know that nothing you do for the Lord is ever useless."* If you don't know what to give them, then walk them through this book with you. Take everything that you've learned and make it your own. Teach others how to belong, how to shed, how to develop, and how to change. You have everything that you need.

ACKNOWLEDGEMENTS

I thank my husband, Michael, for empowering me to share the hardest parts of my story for the betterment of other women. I love you.

I thank Kesha Royster, my mentor, who encouraged me to have tough and honest conversations with the people that I love. In the process of writing this book, I was able to shed, develop, and change even more. I couldn't have done it without you. You've made an eternal impact in my heart.

I thank Jada Hite, my best friend, who has been my supporter and a shoulder to lean on. Thank you for being patient with me, seeing the darkest parts of me, and loving me the same. Thank you also for editing this book. You're my Aaron.

REFERENCES

WOUND CARE CENTERS
https://www.woundcarecenters.org/article/wound-basics/different-types-of-wounds

SCIENTIFIC AMERICAN
https://www.scientificamerican.com/article/caterpillar-butterfly-metamorphosis-explainer/

BUTTERFLY BUSHES
http://www.butterflybushes. com/monarchmetamorphosis.htm
http://www.butterflybushes.com/monarchmetamorphosis.htm

PURPLE BOOK, *Steve Murrell*

PRAYER GUIDE, *Church of the Highlands*

EMOTIONAL HEALING IN 3 EASY STEPS, *Praying Medic*

ABOUT THE AUTHOR

Amanda Pittman is the wife to Michael Pittman and the mother of two kids, Elijah Apollo (aka BEAN) and Lily Blair (aka Juice Juice). She helps her husband pastor a campus of The Gathering Oasis Church in Atlanta, GA. She is the founder of Confident Woman Co., where she hosts mentorship groups, retreats, conferences and daily encouragement. She is the author of two other books, "Reflecting God's Beauty," and "Love Your First Year of Marriage." Amanda speaks at various conferences, panels, and other church events. Amanda is passionate about Jesus and encouraging women to pursue His best for their lives. Her favorite simple pleasures in life include coffee in the morning, cuddles with her family, and words of affirmation.

Instagram + Twitter:
@amandaapittman

Facebook:
Amanda Pittman

YouTube:
www.youtube.com/ThePittmansNow

Websites:
www.amandaapittman.com
www.confidentwomanco.com

Made in the USA
Coppell, TX
21 May 2020